Varmint Q

Other books by Charles Boer:
The Odes (poems)
The Homeric Hymns (translation)

VARMINT

CHARLES BOER, 1939

Illustrated with 28 original woodcuts by
David Hayes.

THE **SWALLOW PRESS** INC.

CHICAGO

Published by
The Swallow Press Incorporated
1139 South Wabash Avenue
Chicago, Illinois 60605

This book is printed on 100% recycled paper

LIBRARY OF CONGRESS CATALOG NO. 74-189194
ISBN Cloth 0572-9
      Paper 0573-7

Some of these poems appeared earlier in *Io* and *Stash*.

for John and Glenis Lobb

Contents

An Invocation to
John Greenleaf Whittier
as an Aside from the Author

You were so sure
of *yourself*
you threw your presentation
copy of
Leaves of Grass into
the fire.
You were the only poet
in the whole of your
not very illustrious century
who did not cross the Atlantic Ocean
in search of
Culture.
You felt that he who wanders widest
lifts no more
of beauty's jealous veil than he
who from his doorway sees
the miracle
of flowers and trees. *Tra la!*
And you were never fooled,
as, god, how many others,
by the enticement of
art, saying,
"No doubt your picture galleries at Florence
are beautiful with art
but nothing like the pictures of God
hung over all our hills."
And once when a man in a neighboring town
wrote you, begging for money,
and threatening to blow his brains out

if he didn't get any
you wrote back saying
"I don't believe you have any brains to blow out."

You who could live so long a bachelor
with all those nineteenth century single women
once your mother died,
with your sister Elizabeth,
and then when she died
with your brother Matthew's daughter,
Lizzie, and then with your cousin,
Abby Woodman, and then with Miss Johnson
and with Phoebe Woodman,
and at Celia Thaxter's house
in the Isle of Shoals
and at Elmfield with Sarah Abbie Gove
and you had 84 years of it,
the women, the hills,
you had to be a poet of narrative
in that all too lyric age.

And though you praised the likes of
Lydia Sigourney, the rage of Hartford,
it was not, I know,
for her confessional poems—
"all my pretty ones"
as she would so wantonly call them,
it was for the same reason
Hartford named a street for her,
which was simply because she knew
you, because she was your friend,
and if they thought, smugly,
they were alone with America,
those improbable friends,
surely you were not, Whittier,
you who used to leave as your calling-card
a green leaf
found in the yard of anyone

not lucky enough to be home
when you so rarely deigned to call.

It was such an obvious touch,
so simple, so artless and natural,
only you could have gotten away with it.
People gave you so much credit
for so little.

And that your own Barbara Frietchie was the one
who waved that Union flag so hard you said
when it was really, now, my own
Mary Quantrell who waved that flag,
this was not anything to them

or you, in the long run,
though it may have destroyed Mary Quantrell
that day. Was there no urgency for truth
in your century either?

And from Mary in Frederick, Maryland,
you moved on to Kansas matters
and the Border Wars, sending your songs
west, to be sung by the emigrants:
> *We cross the prairie as of old*
> *the pilgrims crossed the sea*
> *to make the West as they the East*
> *the homestead of the free*

I have crossed with you, John,
I have sung with you now:
> *We in suffering, they in crime,*
> *wait the just award of time,*
> *wait the vengeance that is due,*
> *not in vain a heart shall break,*
> *not a tear for freedom's sake*
> *fall unheeded: God is true.*
> *While the flag with stars bedecked*
> *threatens where it should protect,*
> *and the Law shakes hands with crime,*
> *what is left us but to wait,*
> *match our patience to our fate*
> *and abide the better time?*

I have waited too, John,
now much longer than you waited,
though we all waited much too long:
> *Well to suffer is divine,*
> *pass the watchword down the line,*
> *pass the countersign: Endure,*
> *not to him who rashly dares,*
> *not to him who nobly bears,*
> *is the victor's garland sure*

4

We have endured, Greenleaf,
though the Law's vicious grip
hurts even worse,
but you have endured as well,
and even cities are named for you now,
Whittier, California, is named for you,
birthplace of the thirty-seventh president
of these still United States:

> —a prouder memory lingers round
> the birthplace of this man here
> than that which haunts the refuge found
> by Arthur's mythic Guinevere
> O hills that watched his boyhood's home,
> O earth and air that nursed him, give
> in this memorial semblance room
> to him who shall its bronze outlive
> and thou, o land he loved, rejoice
> that in the countless years to come
> whenever Freedom needs a voice
> these sculptured lips shall not be dumb

Oh you were witty,
but the author of *Snowbound* was
Whittier,
as schoolboys used to mock,
they used you,
as I use you now, sure,
as only you now can be used,
who once wrote a poem
to the memory of Charles B. Storrs,
late president himself
of Western Reserve College,
who died you said at his post of duty,
in Cleveland, Ohio,
overworn by his strenuous labors
with tongue and pen
in the cause of Human Freedom,

while I, Charles Boer,
a graduate of that same college,
and a native of that same city,
this afternoon find in the mailbox
on my porch in Storrs, Connecticut,
of all places,
a green leaf, oh John!

Was it yours?
Did you call and find me out,
as so many do these days?
How I would have enjoyed your visit,
you who had so much to say,
so much story to tell,
you are the only poet we'll read anymore.

Ancestors

They endowed him with depravity, bestowed upon him the portion of degeneracy. In cruelty and a thirst for blood he towered above the men of his time. Somewhere of old his ancestors ate the sour grapes which set his teeth on edge. In him was exemplified the terrible and immutable law of heredity. He grew into the gory monster whose baleful shadow falls upon all who share the kindred blood. He made his name a Cain's mark and a curse to those condemned to bear it. The blight of it must fall upon remote generations, those yet unborn and innocent, so inexorable are the decrees of fate and nature. Because of him widows wailed, orphans cried, maidens wept, as they lifted the lifeless forms of loved ones from bloody fields and bore them reeking to untimely graves.

—WILLIAM ELSEY CONNELLEY

Uncle Jesse married Mary Lane,
daughter of Seth Lane,
foremost citizen of
Hagerstown, Maryland,
with plenty of money
for his daughter to inherit,
at age 21, from the bank
of Hagerstown, Maryland,
but she married Uncle Jesse
at age 20, so Uncle Jesse
pressed the bank
of Hagerstown, Maryland
to give them the money early,
and the bank did in fact
give them the money early,
but when she turned 21,
a year later, Uncle Jesse
tried to collect again,

7

insisting that the bank
had no legal right
to pay so early

Uncle Jesse bought a grocery store
with the money
in Williamsport, Maryland
but the business failed so
he went to New York
where he pretended to be
the son of a well-known Virginia merchant
so they let him buy on credit
a whole ship full of merchandise
which he then sent
to Baltimore
but they caught him
and he declared himself bankrupt
though it was no use
this was fraud, sir,
they said, and they put him in prison
where for six months
his beautiful wife,
the former Mary Lane,
shared his cell

And when he was released
Uncle Jesse went to
St. Louis
where he was soon in jail again,
this time for counterfeiting
and when he was released
he sailed to
Cincinnati
but while on the boat
he committed forgery again
but got away this time
and so he went
to New Orleans

where his wife became ill
because he beat her
so he proceeded to
take her home to
Maryland
but on the boat
he committed forgery again
and they caught him
and they put him in the jail
in Cincinnati
for seven months
until his wife,
the former Mary Lane,
was able to put up bail
which he then forfeit
by leaving town
and deserting her

Uncle Jesse then went
to Hagerstown
where he was caught for
committing forgery again
but he escaped
to Pennsylvania
where he committed forgery
and was sentenced to three years

And Uncle Jesse's wife,
the aforesaid Mary Lane,
divorced him
while he was in this prison
and though he was very angry
at this action on her part
and though he threatened
to kill her,
he didn't when he got out
but instead he married again,
this time to a lady

from Pennsylvania
but no sooner was he married again
than he committed forgery again
and got seven more years

Mary Lane
who for these years was
Mary Quantrell
had married again
and was now Mary Cowton
of Cumberland, Maryland,
this was in 1848,
and Uncle Jesse was released
this year and went
to Cumberland, Maryland
to Mary's apartment where
he told her her hour had come,
that is what he said,
and he grabbed her throat,
he threw her to the floor,
he placed his knee on her breast
and he shot her in the face
with his pistol

But the pistol misfired
so he drew his knife
but before he could kill her
the neighbors broke in
and he was caught
and put in prison for two years
until he was finally pardoned
and told to get out of this state,
will you, and never return

                    This was your uncle, Q.,
                    Uncle Jesse Duncan Quantrell,
                    who called himself
                    "Doctor Hayne"

And if a man is not responsible
for his relatives,
what is a man
responsible for, Q.,
in addition, that is,
to what he thinks of as his
self, to which,
with another name,
so easily
he gives up all claims
and responsibilities?
(As for you, Q.,
who decided to call your self
Charlie—the irrepressible Charlie Hart—
were you merely being irresponsible?)

Captain Thomas Quantrell moved
to Washington
where he died of apoplexy—
he was stricken directly in front of
The Treasury Building
and died suddenly,
no doubt at the thought
of all that money
inside and no way to get it out—
a kind of constipation, is it not?
the heart cannot take sometimes
what even the mind
is willing to resolve.

There was, as well,
Uncle Archibald Quantrell,
who married Miss Mary Sands
who was 32, in 1862.
She was a Union girl,
for the Union forever.
They lived in
Frederick, Maryland.

11

In September of 1862
Stonewall Jackson
was passing through
Frederick
on his way to
Harper's Ferry.
And as the general and his men
passed in front of
Mary's house
she stood there,
at the gate,
with her daughter, Virginia,
waving *Union* flags
at these rebel soldiers
passing through the streets
of her town,
Frederick.
The soldiers ordered her to
thrown down those flags,
and they took their swords
and they cut one flag
out of the hands
of Mary's daughter,
Virginia.
She picked it up
and waved it again
and the soldiers ordered her to
throw down that flag
and they cut the flag
out of her hands again.
Mary then picked up
the *biggest* Union flag
she had on hand
and waved that—
so that the soldiers started
applauding her,
the officers even
started applauding her,

and one officer saluted her,
not her flag, and said,
"To you, madam,
not to your flag!"
by which he meant
it doesn't matter
what your flag means
though I am ready
to kill you
for what your flag means
but what matters really
is that you wave a flag
that hard
for the sake of
waving a flag hard.

But it was a poet,
wouldn't you know, it was
John Greenleaf Whittier
who got the whole thing wrong,
who botched
the whole simple story,
and said it was
Barbara Frietchie
who waved that flag
when it was not,
it was Mary Quantrell,
wife of Uncle Archibald Quantrell
of Frederick, Maryland.

"Shoot if you must
this old gray head,"
he said Barbara Frietchie
said to Stonewall Jackson's men,
"but spare
your country's flag
she said."
But neither Barbara
nor Mary said this,
this is what Whittier
said Barbara said.
Barbara Frietchie was asleep
at the time, bedridden
with age of all things,
two blocks west of
where Stonewall Jackson's army
was passing through
Frederick.

The poet,
John Greenleaf Whittier,
says he got his information
as to Barbara Frietchie
"from Mrs. E.D.E.N. Southworth

14

the well-known novelist"—
but it is clear
he did not get all the facts
from this well-known novelist.
He could have been more careful
of his information
with a woman of letters like
Mrs. E.D.E.N. Southworth
the well-known novelist.
        (Ah, Q.,
        you thought you knew
        the mystery of names,
        their value in directing
        and redirecting our lives
        in mutual extensions
        of time and place,
        the flag-waving
        poem-singing
        credible dimensions
        of this fake heroine
        of whom ever so vainly
        her countrymen sing,
        and continue to sing,
        via this wayward poet's error.)
Mary Quantrell
never forgot the injustice
this poet did her,
and she protested
to her death
that she was the one,
"I was the one,"
she said, "who waved that flag."
Her brother,
whose name was
of all things,
George Sands,
was a member of the legislature
of Maryland.

He was not
the George Sands,
the well-known novelist,
as how could he be
that well-known woman,
but somewhere
in this imagination
of novelists and poets
there could have been
a crossing of wires
by which Mary's wrong
imaginatively
could have been
straightened out.
Only the imagination
is, probably, real.

"Shoot if you must,"
Mary should have said.

   And that your father, Q.,
   should die of consumption,
   that was no tragedy—
   there was no tragedy in
   this West, in this case Ohio,
   did not most Ohio fathers die
   of consumption anyway?
   consumed by the land itself
   or even by other Ohioans?

After he married
Miss Caroline Cornelia Clarke
(your mother's parents given,
as the poets of that day,
to an excess of alliteration)
he wrote a book
called "Lightning Calculator"
(thinking, was he, of his son?)

and published it
along with another he wrote,
"The Tinman's Guide"
(thinking again of his son?
was he thinking of you, Q.?)
and he published these two books
with funds he had stolen
from the school of
Canal Dover, Ohio,
of which he was a trustee,
being the principal no less
of the school, and he stole
this money from the school
to publish these books,
but a man named Beeson
discovered this theft
and reported it to the town,
and the father said
he would kill that man,
that Beeson,
and one night,
late in autumn,
he entered Beeson's house
with a cocked derringer
in his hand, but Beeson
at the time was sitting
by the fire
heating the point
of a large iron poker
which, when hot,
he intended to plunge
into a cup of cider
which he held in his hand
(a very common Ohio method
for the treatment of cider
and other liquors)

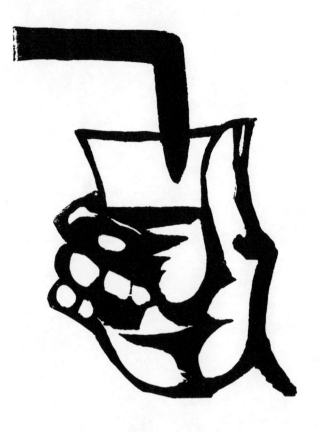

and when the father entered
Beeson's house,
Beeson got up
and struck him on the head
with the poker
before he could shoot
and the father fell
unconscious to the floor,
a long gash in his scalp,
and the neighbors had to come in
and carry the father out
of Beeson's house
where he was sometime recovering
from the blow.

He died December 7, 1854.
He was a good teacher,
they said, and much loved
by his pupils.
        (And you, Q.,
        who would be a teacher
        yourself in the same school,
        at 16, what did he teach you,
        what could anybody teach you,
        the original tin man,
        guide or not, before
        even that other
        that would find his home
        as you, in Kansas, that Oz,
        that wizardless land
        so full of tin men
        that you would soon
        burn to the ground,
        imagine! you burned Oz
        to the ground, the emerald city!
        Lawrence, Kansas!
        where there was no fire department
        capable of the likes of you—
        did he teach you to do that?)

As for the mother,
she once said of her son,
"he always respected Woman
wherever he met them."
And she defended her son to the last.
If the people
of Canal Dover, Ohio
said "hard things"
about her son
it was, she said, because there was
"a dreadful Low class of people there
who delight in slander and Lies
and if God ever makes another Hell

he aught to make it there,"
(in Ohio? Mrs. Quantrell,
are you saying God should make it
in Ohio?) "Sink it in the bottomless Pit
and put all the Liars in it.
It would not be
any too large," she said,
"for all Dover liars."

But you fixed her,
Q., you never sent her
a penny, even when
the cash was coming in
from the Kansas banks
and farms you robbed,
you kept telling her
you were teaching school
and everybody knows
schoolteachers don't make anything.

After the demise
of her son, the mother went to
Missouri
where the old gang was hiding out,
and they entertained her there,
in their homes,
they took care of her,
until she started stealing money
from them, which she said
her son had left with them
for her. They called her a hellcat
and threw her out.

Her son left his money
at his death
with instructions
that a monument
was to be erected to himself.
And to a former mistress
he left some money too,
with instructions
to "start a house of ill fame"
in St. Louis.
That is what he said.
His mother
never believed this.

But William Scott
could believe it.
He was the first
biographer
of Varmint Q.:

It is Wednesday,
December 7, 1887.
I go to the
St. John's Catholic Cemetery
in Louisville, Kentucky
and call on Mrs. Bridget Scally,
the widow in charge.
Twenty-two years before this,
on death day,
the 6th of June, 1865
the body of
William Clark Quantrell
(the guerilla)
was buried here, in secret,
and no mound was raised
over the grave, and dish-water
and other slop
was thrown over it,
not, as one would think,
to dishonor it, but
to hide it, to
keep the body
from being stolen.

Hello, Mrs. Scally,
how are you? Oh,
your husband has died,
I'm sorry to hear that.
I've brought Mrs. Quantrell with me,
you remember her, the mother
of the guerilla?
She wants to see the grave

and she wants to remove
the bones and place them
in the family cemetery
in Ohio, but
if you won't let her do that,
could she at least
dig up the bones
and place them in
a zinc box?

It is cloudy,
a drizzly day and
uncomfortable and
Louis Wertz, the gravedigger,
does not like to do
this kind of job
but I give him a dollar
in addition to the
two dollars and fifty cents
which I give to Mrs. Scally
and in about an hour
at about 3 in the afternoon
the bones are uncovered.
They lie in a natural position,
though the top of the skull
is uppermost, instead of
lying on the back part.
Every vestige of a coffin
is gone, except for a rotten piece
size of a man's hand.
His hair has slipped off
in a half circle
around the skull,
and is bleached yellow.
A small part of
a government army sock
is on one of the foot bones.
A part of the backbone

and the ribs
are so decayed
that they crumble to pieces,
but most of the other bones are
okay.

Mrs. Quantrell
could not come this far
because of the weather
so I put the bones
in a small box
and put them back
in the grave, at the top,
lightly covered over.

I take the skull,
with Mrs. Scally's permission,
and wrap it in newspapers
and take it back to the hotel
to show to Mrs. Quantrell,
the mother of the guerilla.
She is much affected by it.
She identifies
a chipped side tooth
in lower jaw
on right side.
But she will not let me
take the skull back
to Mrs. Scally,
because it must be buried,
she says, in a zinc box
in Ohio.
She wants the rest of him too
buried in Ohio.

So I carefully wrap the skull
and place it in a basket
and I check it
at the hotel desk.
She then insists
that I go dig up the bones
without Mrs. Scally knowing it
and place them in a zinc box
for burial in Ohio.
I do not approve
of this deception,
but Mrs. Quantrell says
she will smooth things over
with Mrs. Scally afterwards.
She says
she cannot stand the thought
of forms and proofs and red tape
to get the bones out.

I go back
and get the bones out
and place them in
a zinc box
and take them
for burial, to Ohio.
Mrs. Quantrell
then goes to see Mrs. Scally
but she puts all the blame
on me!
In this way
she reconciles
Mrs. Scally,
who agrees finally
that secrecy
is the best policy
and that the end
justifies the means.

FEB. 6., 1889

"Mrs. Quantrell,
I don't see why
you have written me
one or two such letters
as you have
since I left you
to bury the bones
in Ohio.
I had been your friend
in many dark days
when you needed one;
and I always took your part
and defended you.
After I came home,
you wrote me a very unkind letter,
accusing me
of having photographed
the men at Blue Springs,

and sending the photographs
to the Police Gazette
to be ridiculed.
I wrote you back at once
that I had not one
of their photographs!
had not taken any,
and had never written a line
to the Police Gazette
or any other paper;
and to prove it all,
I got a copy
of the Police Gazette
and sent it to you.
I thought that would convince you
that you was mistaken,
but you never answered the letter."

FEB. 24TH 1889

"I cannot understand
what you mean
by saying you were
such a great friend
to me in my dark days
when I needed one,
and always took my part
and defended me.
I don't know of
any very dark days
I ever had . . ."

Birth of a Varmint

There was once a boy
who lived in Ohio
who shot a pig
through the tip of an ear
to make it run
and hear it squeal.
The boy would laugh
when the pig would squeal.
AHREEK! AHREEK!
The pig would squeal,
the boy would laugh.
Sometimes
the boy would nail a snake
to the top of a tree
and then he would watch it squirm.
SQUEEUSH! SQUEEUSH!
The snake would squirm
and the boy would laugh.
The boy would stick his knife in cows
that stood by the side of the road.
AHMUH! AHMUH!
The cows would groan
and the boy would laugh.
The boy would stab horses
and he would torture dogs and cats.
Of the boy's brother
it is said that
he would chase after cows
on his crutches
and stab them.
Then the boy,
or his brother,
would laugh.

There would be laughter
everywhere.

In the village of the boy,
which was called Dover,
there was a church and it was
far off from everything else
and the public road ran by its door,
and the pasture for the cows of this village
lay beyond this church,
and along the public road,
and one day the boy was walking his cow
past the church on this public road
when the keeper of the church,
who was a girl,
came to ring the evening bell
for that day, and since
this belfry was entered
through a door with a thick shutter
that was secured by a heavy lock
that was turned with an enormous key,
when the boy saw the door
of the belfry standing open
and when he heard the bell clanging
he knew that the girl was in the belfry,
and, further, that she was alone,
so the boy closed the door of the belfry
quietly and he locked it
and he took the key
and threw it in the water of the creek,
which was called Sugar Creek,
in Ohio, and the girl was locked in
the belfry for one whole day without food
or water (though she should have known enough
to keep ringing the bell from the belfry),
and when the members of the church
found the girl in the belfry
the next day, they were so enraged

they offered a reward
of one hundred dollars
for the apprehension of
"this criminal".

Then the boy moved to Kansas
where he told the people of that state
that if they ever went to Ohio
they could collect one hundred dollars
if they told the members of the church
that he was the boy
who locked the girl in the belfry.

The boy was in the West
only a few months
before he tired of it.
He wanted to go back to Ohio.
"I am tired of the West already,"
the boy said, "and I do not think
I shall stay in it
very much longer than I can help.
I want to go back to Ohio."

WEDNESDAY AUGUST 8TH, 1855
MENDOTA, LA SALLE CO ILLINOIS

Dear Mother,

I arrived here about half past two o'clock this afternoon safe and
sound. My box is not here but I expect it tomorrow. We traveled
day and night ever since we started not having stopped half an
hour at one place. Tomorrow I am going to hunt something to do.
We are both well except that Mary was looking out of the window
of the car while we were going along the shore of Lake Michigan
when a spark of fire flew in her eye and made it a little sore. But
that will be well in a day or so. We did not have any trouble with
our trunks at all. I have $6 of my money left and maybe the next
time I write I will send a little along. I am about 600 miles from
home.

This country is a great deal different from Ohio for miles around I can see nothing but tall grass. There is not much Fruit here although I have seen ripe peaches at the cars for sale: but corn, potatoes, cabbage are plenty. We have stopped at Marys Aunts Mrs. Cross but I wont stay here but a day or so. There are two schools here   probably I can get one of them. Well I believe that is all this time   the next time I will write more

One day the boy shot a man
in Mendota, Illinois
whom he said had knocked him down
with the intention of robbing him.
But the man had not knocked him down,
and had no intention of robbing him.

How did the boy from Ohio
get to Kansas? It was with the help
of some friends from Ohio,
whose names were Beeson and Torrey,
who lived in an old cabin
of small dimensions,
across the back of which
was a platform
where Beeson and Torrey slept,
while the son of Beeson and the boy
slept on blankets
that were spread before the fire
on the floor, but the boy
kept hogging the blankets
and so the son of Beeson
was cold every night,
even though Beeson and Torrey
told the boy to stop
hogging the blankets,
so one night Beeson said to his son,
"Son, you sleep with Torrey
and I will sleep with the boy,"
but during that night

Beeson dreamed he was in danger
and he woke up suddenly
to find the boy standing over him
in the act of plunging
a long Mexican dagger
into his heart,
so Beeson got up
and took away the dagger
from the boy, then took a switch
which he laid on
until the boy cried.

STANTON KANSAS TER.
MAY 16, 1857

My dear Mother,

We have had a very backward spring here; but from what news
we get they have had a worse time in Ohio and all of the eastern
states. Although the trees are all green here, and the prairie looks
like a field of wheat. I suppose by the time you receive this letter
Grandfather will be there if he is not there already. If he is there
or not, I want you if possible to sell out there and let me have part
of the money out here to procure a home for us all, consisting of
160 acres of land; either prairie or timber, or half of each, or almost any proportion of each one would wish to have. If you can
do this by any possible means do so and we can move here this
fall and be much more comfortably situated than in Dover, or any
place else east of Kansas. Older heads than mine may try to persuade you that this is not the case, but it is so, for all is peace and
quietness here now, and it will remain so without doubt. Why, not
less than 50,000 people from the North have come into the Territory this spring so that Kansas will soon be a State among States
and able to maintain her own rights.

If you can persuade Grandfather to let us sell out root and branch
it will be undoubtedly the best thing you could do. Then we will
be square with the world and able to say our soul is our own without being contradicted. Is not this worth sacrificing something
for? I think it is, and so you will, I know.

33

If we cannot do this I will not stay here longer than fall, for I can make much more money in the States at teaching than by hard work here. I am here now as an agent to get a home for us all, which I can do if there is not too much opposition. I have thought over the matter, and Mr. Torrey says it is the best I can do. Do not let anybody persuade you out of this until they produce better grounds for not doing as I have said than I have for doing so. It is the best we can do, and everybody will say so who reasons the case well.

If you can have such good luck as to dispose of the property, you can take out letters of administration yourself. If not, Grandfather, or some one in whom you can confide. If the thing can be done, do it as soon as you can for it will be all the better.

I will tell you now how we get along here. We live on side meat—bacon about four inches thick; corn cakes, beans, few dried apples occasionally, and fish and squirrels when we can get them which we have pretty good luck doing. Our house is built of round logs with a fire place made partly of stone; a floor made of puncheon—that is split boards about 3 inches thick. Our furniture consists of 2 stools made out of puncheon, 3 trunks and a table made when we wish to use it by putting a board (which we found in the river) across the 2 trunks. Our walls are decorated with guns, boots, side meat, skillets, surveying chain etc. The only job that we have to do that we all dislike, is dishwashing which Mr. Beeson is doing now. We have to take turn about at it; no one will do it more than twice in succession. Our stock consists of 3 yoke of cattle, six pigs and about 2 dozen chickens. We will have by fall 3 times as much stock if we have good luck. All I want is for the rest of you to be here, and we will live twice as fast.

One day the boy steals
a yoke of oxen
from Beeson
and some blankets and pistols
from Torrey.
Beeson looks everywhere
for his oxen.
He thinks at first
they have strayed.
When Beeson can't find his oxen
he concludes
the boy has stolen them.
He accuses the boy
of having stolen his oxen.
He tells the boy
that if he doesn't show him
where they are hidden
right now
he will shoot him down
like a dog.

He orders the boy to move
on pain of instant death
to where he has hidden the oxen.
He puts the muzzle of his gun
to the boy's back
and they start moving
down the path
to where he has hidden the oxen.
The boy leads the way
into a thicket
in the river bottom
where the oxen are yoked
and chained to a tree.
The oxen are so weak
from starvation
that they cannot stand.
Beeson feeds his oxen
for two days
before he can drive them home.

STANTON, KANSAS
JULY 9TH, 1857

I have taken my atlas and went to the bank of the river in the
shade, to write. Everything feels and looks happy; the wood is
full of birds of every kind, seeing which can sing best and sweet-
est. The fish are playing in the water of the river, which is clear
as crystal; and the squirrel bounds from tree to tree, till seeing me
he stops, and after eyeing me curiously, then scampers on again
till I almost envy him his happiness.

Quantrell was
a gambler.

While sauntering on through
a big gambling tent
a day or so after payday,
watching the fluctuations of fortune

at the various tables,
someone remarked:
"Here comes Charley Hart."
He was 22 or 23 years of age,
about 5 feet 10 inches in height,
with an ungraceful, slouchy walk,
and by no means prepossessing
in features. He had been patronizing
Judge Carter's store,
and he struck it rich
for his clothes all seemed new.
A pair of high-heeled calf-skin boots
of small size, bottoms of trousers
tucked into boot-tops,
a navy pistol
swinging from his waist belt,
a fancy blue flannel shirt,
no coat,
a colored silk handkerchief
tied loosely around his neck,
yellow hair
hanging nearly to the shoulders,
topped out by
the inevitable cowboy hat.
As he entered the tent
he carried in his left hand
a colored silk handkerchief,
gathered by the four corners,
which apparently contained coin.
Advancing to one of the tables
where the banker was dealing Monte,
he set the handkerchief on the table
and opened it out,
showing the contents to be
gold coins, and seemingly in bulk
about equal to the stacks of gold coins
tiered up on the table
in front of the banker.

Hart then asked:
"Take a nap, pard?"
meaning
would the banker accept a bet
of Hart's pile
against the dealer's,
on the turn of a card.
The banker accepted the challenge,
shuffled the cards,
passed the deck to Hart to cut,
then threw out the lay-out of six cards
in a column of twos style.
Hart then set his handkerchief of gold
on a card, at the same time

drawing his pistol,
"Just to insure fair play,"
he remarked, seeing that
the banker had his gun
lying on the table
convenient to his right hand.
Keeping his eye on the banker's hands,
to make sure that the deal was done
on the square, Hart said,
"Now deal."
Turning the deck face up,
the banker drew the cards off.
Hart's card won.
As the dealer looked up
with a muttered oath
he found himself
looking into the muzzle
of Hart's pistol.
"Back out,"
said Hart quietly.
"Don't even touch your pistol."
The banker did as directed,
while Hart
picked out the twenties,
tens, fives, and two-and-a-half pieces
and tossed them into his handkerchief.
There still remained on the table
a double handful of small silver,
and a handful of gold dollars.
Sweeping this small stuff into his hands
Hart said, "I don't carry
such chicken feed as that,"
and he tossed the small coins
up in the air
and let the crowd scramble for them.
Then he handed the dejected banker
a twenty dollar gold piece
and said: "There, pard,

is a stake for you."
And gathering up his
plethoric
handkerchief
he meandered on
seeking new banks to bust.

TUSCARORA LAKE
JAN. 22D 1858

Friend William,

I have come to the conclusion to write to you again. You wrote
to me last summer and I answered it shortly afterward; but, not
having received one afterwards, I came to the conclusion that you
had never received it; for at that time letters frequently were mis-
laid and lost.

But when one does sit down to write here, he hardly knows what
to say; for situated as we are, and away from any town we are at
more of a loss for news etc. than you gentlemen in the city there.
I have left Col Torreys and now live with the rest of the Dover
boys here. George Hildt is in Dover ere this and if you see him
tell him we are all well and that the claim North of mine was
jumped last Monday by a young fellow from Ind.

About the last election here is this 10,126 votes against the Lecompton swindle and 6000 for it, of which 3000 if not more were
illegal. I saw the Ohio Democrat here yesterday which had
some what I call D_____n lies about Kansas and I would like to
tell the editor so to his face. He said Jim Lane, (as good a man
as we have here) was fighting with U.S. Troops at Fort Scott, he
was there but did no fighting; his presence is enough to frighten
100 Missourians. The settlers shot two men and wounded 4 or 5
but in self defence, it is a pity they had not shot every Missourian
that was there. The democrats here are the worst men we have for
they are all rascals, for no one can be a democrat here without being one; but the day of their death is fast approaching and they
will be like the jews be scattered to the four winds of the earth
and a guilty look which will always betray them.

40

If you are in the printing office yet tell the editor if he wants any subscribers in Kansas he must do a little better than he has done, for the boys here will hardly use it when they go back of the house.

If you know where George Scott is tell him to write to me or if he wants to get a farm of nothing to come here as soon as he can; for there are good chances here now, tell him I am safe for 160 acres of land and that I will insure the same to him if he comes here in 8 or 10 weeks; and you too Billy $40 will Bring him here yes 30 if he is economical and I will insure anyone $1.50 a day if he wants to work, and Friend William if you want land here is the only place to get it cheap and you had better come if you want any. Tell George if he wants to come, to come by railroad to Jefferson City, Mo. and then shoulder his carpet sack and foot it to Independence and from there to Little Santa Fe and then to Olathe Johnson County K.T. which is six day walk, if you see any Boys around Dover who want to come tell them what I have written.

We have the finest weather imaginable well to tell you the truth the grass has been growing on the prairie all winter or during the season we call winter and we have no rainy or wet weather either.

Last week I helped to kill a deer and since I have been here I have killed myself 2 antelope and one deer and about 25 Wild Turkeys and geese and before you see me in Ohio I will have killed buffalo for they are plenty about 100 miles west of us now and those who have killed them say it is fine sport at least if I keep my health I will try it. This is the place to hunt there is more game to be seen in one day here than in a whole year there.

About the girls I cannot say as much as you could but this is certain a man can have his choice for we have all kinds and colors here Black White and Red. But to tell you which I like the best is a mixture of the two latter colors if properly brought up for they are both rich and good looking and I think go ahead of your Dover gals far enough. Em Walton would pass very well for a squaw if she was better looking but I think from present appearances John Diehl will squaw her next fall or winter and that will

41

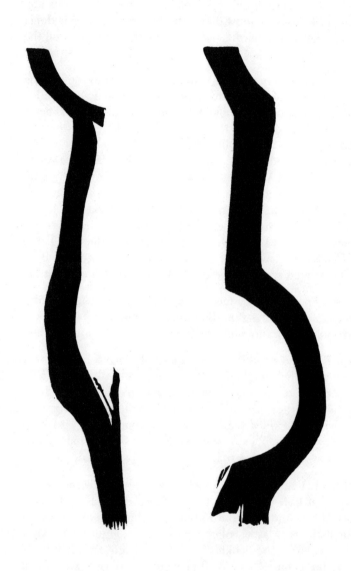

42

bleach her a little probably. When you write tell me all about the girls and especially yours and my fair one that used to be in years past, if she is around yet. You and the rest of the boys there must attend to the girls well while we are here in Kansas, and tell them we are all going to marry squaws and when they die we are coming to old Dover for our second wives so that they must not despair.

I must close. Now write soon give me all the news my love to the boys and girls and oblige

Your obedient S.
W. C. QUANTRILL

Q. goes
to the Great Salt Lake City
and is never so surprised
as when he finds
how people live in cities and towns here:
"You go in their towns and cities,"
Q. says, "and you find the purest and clearest
of springwater
coming from the snow-capped mountains
and running on either side of the streets
and through their lots
in small but rapid streams
carrying off the filth
and keeping everything as fresh as it was
when spring first opened."

Q. goes
to an agricultural fair
that the Mormons hold
and is never so surprised:
"For it equaled any of our county fairs,"
Q. says, "in everything
except fine horses, and cattle,
and peaches, apples, plums, grapes
and indeed all kinds of fruits and vegetables

equaled
and in some instances far surpassed
anything in the east that ever I had seen;
especially the vegetables,
onions as large as a saucer,
potatoes, beets, radishes, carrots, parsnips etc.
were larger than any I had ever seen;
and then the needlework was very fine,
and the picture gallery was splendid
and the specimens of their manufactures
were very fine indeed,
and then a very fine brass and string band
entertained us
an hour or so
every half day
very agreeably."

Q. does not think
of getting married yet,
"although every man here,"
he says, "has from 5 to 8 wives
and the rich have from 12 to 20
and Brigham has at present 43."

LAWRENCE,
JULY 30TH/59

My dear Mother,

It has been some time since I wrote to you, and I am now a long ways distant from the place I last wrote to you. I have seen some pretty hard and scaly times, both from cold weather and starvation and the Indians and I am one of 7 out of a party of 19 who started from Salt Lake city for the Gold Mines of Pikes Peak, which are talked of all over the country and undoubtedly *the* Humbug of all Humbugs; I say so because I spent two months in the Gold Region haveing my own experience and that of a number with whom I was acquainted to prove it conclusively. there is more or less gold scattered over a country about 40 miles in width running from the mountains east and about 200 miles long running with the mountains but not in quantities paying of 1.00 per day in the best diggings. I dug out $54.34 and worked 47 days which money hardly paid my board and expenses. I am now in Lawrence after having spent over $300 and many a day and night when I expected either to be killed or freeze to death and at last when nearly in the settlements to have my horse and all taken from me and a companion of mine shot in 3 different places and left for dead and all that saved my head was I was out hunting away from the camp about a mile and a half and hearing the firing hurried to camp in time to see the indians driving off our horses and my friend lying on the ground apparently dead but still breathing with difficulty having been shot 3 times, his leg broke below the knee shot in the thigh with 7 iron slugs and last shot through the body with an arrow which I first thought would kill him but he lives yet and if taken care of properly will be as well as ever in 6 or 8 weeks. I hardly know what to do at present nor where to go but in my next letter I will be able to tell you some more   I think my friend and myself will make government pay us for our losses by the Indians if possible when he gets well   You would hardly know me if you were to see me I am so weather beaten and rough looking that everybody says I am about 25 years of age.

The schoolhouse stood
on the northwest corner
of the southwest quarter
of Section 33, Township 17, Range 22,
of Stanton Kansas.
It cost each student
$2.50 for three months
of a six month term.
The students were:
Thomas F. Roberts and his wife,
Roxey Troxel Roberts,
George Hill Troxel,
Harrison Troxel,
George Shearer,

H. Shearer,
Delama Shearer,
Belle Roberts,
Eliza Roberts,
Flora Roberts,
Mark Updegraff,
Augustus Updegraff,
David Updegraff,
Elzena Williams,
Amanda Williams,
Jefferson Williams,
Polk Williams,
Roger Williams,
Wesley Baker,
Hester Baker,
Adolphus Y. Bennings,
and James Bennings.
William Stockwell
was not a student
in the school, but
he lived near it and
he helped build it
and on Friday nights
he did attend
the spelling school
that Q. taught.
He said that Q. talked in class
for the Free-State side
but took no part in raids
while a teacher in the school;
that he was very quiet;
told of having been across the plains;
dressed neatly;
had peculiar eyes which were blue;
though at times they were
a strange undefinable color;
and the upper lids had a queer look.

Roxey Troxel Roberts
was the daughter
of Frederick Troxel of Kentucky,
who moved to Illinois,
then to Iowa, then to Kansas,
arriving in Osawotomie in 1855.
Roxey said
Q. was a good teacher;
had large light-blue eyes,
a Roman nose,
light complexion, light hair;
that he had peculiar eyes,
· like no other eyes she ever saw,
the upper lids were heavy;
that he talked in class
for the Free-State side
but took no part in the raids
while a teacher.

STANTON, KANSAS TERRI.
JAN. 26TH 1860

My dear Mother,

It is now noon and I again write, for I had to stop when it was time for school to begin. The weather has changed some little since, and ever and anon the sun bursts through the clouds, melting the snow on the roof, and causes the ice clad forest to sparkle and shine like silver, and the storm is gradually passing away, and it seems it has been only a frown which has passed over the heavens, which are now being lit up with glad smiles, and soon all will be pleasant again. And when I look out upon the snow it reminds me again of my mountain trip; and the ex-cruciating pain we suffered from snowblindedness, caused by looking all day on the bright snow; none of us were exempt from this, the sensation is that of having your eyes badly smoked, which lasted for several days, the eyes become inflamed and swollen causing very much pain.

There is no news now I believe at present, all is peace and quietness in the country, and all seems to move on smoothly, but times are hard, and the people complain of the taxes which they have to pay, and indeed they are enormous for such a new country, and under the present form of government are not apt to cease.

You have undoubtedly heard of the wrongs committed in this territory by the southern people, or proslavery party, but when one once knows the facts they can easily see that it has been the opposite party that have been the main movers in the troubles and by far the most lawless set of people in the country. They all sympathize for old J. Brown, who should have been hung years ago, indeed hanging was too good for him. May I never see a more contemptible people than those who sympathize for him. A murderer and a robber, made a martyr of; just think of it.

When you write let me know all that you have time to write about, for I feel anxious to know something about home and the village of my boyhood more than I have been heretofore and I cannot really say why it is so, but I think of it more, and have lately visited it in my dreams, which was quite rare before; it may be because my mind has become more settled, and my mind must be employed in some way, and I suppose that is the most natural. I wish to know all that has happened of note lately, and I would like well to be there and I think I will be, (if I live) in the course of the summer. At least I have made up my mind to that point I suppose all the people about there never think I am coming back again, and that also that I have done wrong in going away at all; this I will acknowledge, but who could have made me believe it at that time, I think no one, for my brain ran so with wild thoughts that I was blind to everything else. I think that I am not the only one, of that failing; only it has, probably been carried to a greater extent in my case than others, and my situation has been different from theirs.

Though I have been quite foolish in my notions of the last three or four years, still I have been taught many a good lesson by them, and think I shall not regret it in after life so much as I do now, for it is now that I feel it the keenest, and can see the whole picture of my doings in one broad sheet, which may be rolled up and laid by to look upon in after life. I have seen a little of the world I know how others manage to keep moving in the vast crowd which is moving ahead; I have seen the means used by different communities to keep body and soul together, I have compared them with each other and find in the end they all amount to the same, with only this difference, that their situations are different, and the ends accomplished are adapted to their situations. this (is all) a good comfortable living, which any person of good health and mind can procure in any country for theirself and two or three others and still have plenty of time for amusement; and this is all we can have in the world.

49

Charley Hart

My first
        real
acquaintance with him
was on the 4th of July
1859.
The people of Lawrence
held what they call
        a celebration
on that day
across the Kansas River
on the Delaware Reserve.
John C. Vaughan then living
        at Leavenworth
came over and made the address
on that day.
I don't know what time it was
but while the judge was speaking
there was an outcry
a little distance off
in the brush
and several of us
ran to see the cause.
There we found
        a white man
lying on the ground
in an unconscious condition
with his head
badly cut
hacked up
by an Indian tomahawk
apparently.
        Quantrell
was one of the first men

to arrive on the spot.
He said he knew
                    the Indian
who committed the assault
he went on to say
that the man had enticed
the Indian's wife
away, and that this was done
for revenge.
                    Quantrell assisted
for an hour or more
in caring for the man
while the doctor was giving
what they call
                    restoratives
to the man
during which time
Q told me
that he started out for Salt Lake
the fall before
                    as a teamster
with some government expedition
against Mormons.
He also went on to say
that he was living
at that time
with Henry Bascom
a Delaware Indian
                    out about
three miles from Lawrence.
Later in the summer
I saw him again
and he said
that he was living
at that time
with George Sarcoxie
another Delaware Indian
out about

five miles from Lawrence
on the reserve.
             John Sarcoxie
was the son of Sarcoxie
chief
of the Delaware Nation.
         And he
John Sarcoxie
was living on Mud Creek
out about
four miles northeast
of Lawrence.
        And Quantrell said
he was
           the detective
for the Delaware Nation.
But he had no occupation
among the Delaware Nation
and he did not work
at anything.
Here is how he spent his time:
he spent
his time
          riding
about the country
on an Indian pony.
He would ride up
to the north ferry landing
on this Indian pony.
         The ferry
was established by John Baldwin
and was the first ferry landing
at Lawrence.
          Quantrell
would make his appearance
at the north ferry landing
at about nine in the morning.
He would hitch

the Indian pony
in the brush
and then go down
to the north ferry landing.
He remained there
until near night
when he would
                remount
the Indian pony
and return
           promptly
to the home
of John Sarcoxie.
The north ferry landing
was a loafing place
for thieves
murderers
kidnappers
and negro-stealers.
Among these were
Old Man McGee
and his two sons
Jacob and Thomas
called Jake and Tom
McGee.
They were from Pennsylvania.
There was a cousin of these
and he was a very hard character
who because of the
                marital calamity
which befell him
            very frequently
was called
"Cuckold Tom"
McGee.
The McGees had a claim
on the Kansas River
out about two miles

East of Lawrence
in the timber
surrounded by almost
impenetrable brakes
and thickets
and in a little clearing
they had there
they had built a cabin
in which they lived.
And living with them
was another cousin
whose name was
Henry McLaughlin
of character equally base
and vicious.
And a constant associate
of these men was
Esau Sager
a border ruffian
and as tough a character
as lived in Kansas Territory.
There were Jack Elliott
John Stropp, Jay Vince
and Frank Baldwin
and they would make raids
these men
into Missouri
to get slaves
or livestock
to kidnap
            a free negro
in Kansas
or plunder people
of property.
All of these men were
in a slight degree
subject to
            Jake Herd.

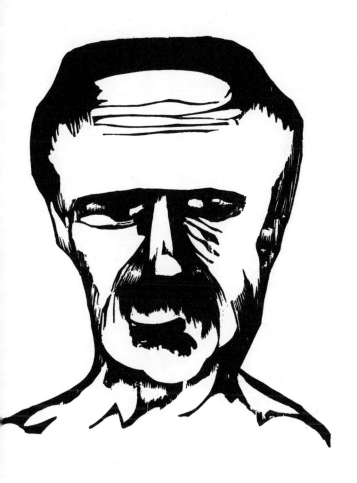

During the winter of 1858–9
several attempts were made
by a gang of
unprincipled fellows
living in and around
Lawrence and Lecompton
to kidnap a number of colored persons
from the city of Lawrence

and its neighborhood
with the intention of selling them
into slavery
in Missouri.
The first attempt was made upon
Charles Fisher
a light mulatto
who kept a barber's shop
in Lawrence.
He was seized
and put into a carriage;
jumping out was chased
and shot at
but managed to evade
the ruffians.
On the next evening
another colored man
William Riley
was seized and carried off
but he also
succeeded in escaping
from the room in which he was
bound and confined
in the house of a man named
Corel
out about two miles
from Lawrence
and he got back to that
city of refuge
            Lawrence.
Two men named
Fry and Goss
the former an old resident
of Lawrence
the latter a stranger
were arrested
            and examined
before a Justice of the Peace

upon the charge of kidnapping.
Sufficient proof of their complicity
was shown
to cause them to be committed
to answer
at the U.S. District Court
but they were released
under a writ
of habeas corpus
issued by Judge Elmore
an appointee
of the Administration
and the largest slaveholder
in Kansas.
This was in October 1858.
At last
the colored people in Lawrence
finding themselves
             in constant danger
applied to the citizens
for protection
in consequence of which application
a meeting was held
in the Court House
to take the matter
into consideration.
As no adequate protection
against the kidnappers
could be assured
to the colored people
if they remained in
             Lawrence
a removal to Iowa
was agreed upon
and some money was raised
to defray the expense.
And it was I
Dr. John Doy

who was solicited
to convey these people
as far as Holton
in Calhoun County
as it was I
who had just returned
from a tour through that section
of Kansas

and it was I
who was best acquainted with the roads
and the people along the roads.
It was I who was considered
the best fitted person for the task
and so I complied with the request
and I agreed to undertake the trip
with my own wagon
and my own horses
which were to be driven
by my own eldest son
Charles Doy
who was then twenty-five years old.
And as it was my wagon
that would not contain
all the passengers
another wagon
and another pair of horses
were obtained
and it was Mr. Clough
who was a young man
who lived near Lawrence
who was engaged to drive them.
The passengers were
eight men
three women
and two children.
And all the adults
except two of the men
showed my son
Charles Doy
their free papers
and all the adults
had their free papers
except these two men
whom we knew to be
                    free men.
One was Wilson Hays

from Cincinnati, Ohio
and the other was Charles Smith
from Brownsville, Pennsylvania.
And it was these two men
who had been employed as cooks
at the Eldredge House
in Lawrence.
It was on the morning
of the 25th of January
that we started out.
I was on horseback
the men walked behind the wagons
the wagons contained the stores
and the women
and the children.
We crossed the Kansas River
at Lawrence
and we traveled
through the Delaware Reservation
towards Oscaloosa.
And it was when we were
out about
twelve miles from Lawrence
and eight from Oscaloosa
and having ascertained
as I supposed
that the road was clear
that I requested the men
to get into the wagons
as we had
a long descent before us
and would go down
at a brisk pace.
And they did so, the men,
and then everybody was in
the wagons except myself
and the wagons were of course
covered and so of course

prevented the men
from seeing what occurred
immediately afterwards
and of course from
defending themselves.
And it was at the bottom of
the hill
on the right of the road
that there was a bluff
from behind which
as we turned it
came out a body of some twenty
or even more
armed and mounted men.
Eleven of these men
approached with rifles
and ordered us to halt.
My son Charles Doy
along with
Wilson Hays
the colored man from Cincinnati
sprang out of my wagon
which was ahead
and shouted
Father, we're stopped!
Shall we shoot?
It was I then who dismounted
and who ran round
to the off side
of the wagon
telling them to hold on
till I ascertained
who the men were
and what the men wanted.
And it was as I advanced
towards the latter
and as I demanded of them
what their business was

that some of them cried out
Shoot him! Shoot him!
and that they aimed their guns
at me.
I told them to shoot me
but not to fire at the wagons
as there were women and children
in the wagons.
I felt perfectly reckless
seeing that
we were overpowered
and that we could do nothing.
And there were five of these
assailants
that I recognized: these were
two young men
named McGee
who lived near Franklin
a fellow named Whitley
who lived in Lawrence
a Dr. Garvin
who was the modern Democratic
postmaster
of that city
and a notorious ruffian
and kidnapper
                    Jake Herd
who lived out about
four miles from Lecompton.
And I spoke to these men
separately
asking if they had any process
against us
that they stopped us
on the highway
but their only replies were
oaths threats and revolvers.
I turned to Whitley and I said

What? You here, Whitley?
Where's your process?
Here it is, he replied
and he put the muzzle
of his revolver
to my head.
You will have to pay for this
I replied.
Then it was that I asked
the others
if they had any papers to show
that any of the colored
people were claimed
as slaves
or if owners were present.
The only replies were
bitter denunciations of us
nigger-thieves
and finally an offer
of 500 dollars
was made from a man
who was a stranger to me
if I would drive the colored people
to the Rialto Ferry
on the Missouri River
opposite Weston.
I told him
no teams of mine should ever be used
to carry a human being
into slavery
with my consent.
You shall go anyhow
damn you,
was his reply.
We don't mean to let you go back
and bring down a gang
of God damned
abolitionists.

63

That's your business
was what I replied.
I should not go
if I could help it.
A portion of the party
then dismounted
and went towards the wagons
the rest keeping their rifles
leveled
upon us.
The men and women were ordered
out and tied
one by one
as they descended from the wagons.
My son Charles Doy
had a gun in his hands
which he discharged
into the air
finding that
resistance was useless.
At the same time
                    Jake Herd
came near shooting himself
as he tried to draw a gun
out of the wagon.
The hammer caught
in some bedding
and the contents of the barrel
passed between his arm
and his body
deflected by a button
that was on his overcoat.
Then it was that I said
I wish to the Lord
it had shot you through the heart
Jake.
And Jake replied
I'll shoot you.

Do so, I replied,
and I'll give you
the best horse I own.
After the colored people
were all tied up
three of the gang seized me
and tried to tie my hands
behind my back
but seeing that my son's arms
were already tied
I broke away from them
and I went up to Herd
and I asked him
to untie my son.
He would not untie my son
so I untied my son myself.
Whereupon Herd
threatened to shoot me
but I paid no attention
to his threats.
And it was then that they realized
that we valued life
cheaper
than they supposed.
So they consented
that my son Charles Doy
and I should go unbound
provided we would go quietly
and promising us that
when we reached the Rialto Ferry
on the Missouri River
opposite Weston
our property would be restored to us
and we would be free
to return
with good pay
for our time and trouble.
We had no choice of course

but to submit.
It was then that I saw
the two colored men
before named
with their arms tied
and I proceeded
to untie them too
telling the kidnappers
that I knew they were
free men.
Our captors were much angered
by our acts and speech
and they held a consultation
as to what should be done with us.
It was Jake Herd
and the McGees
who advised murder, saying
Dead men tell no tales.
The others advised
retreat as they thought
an armed escort
might be expected from Lawrence.
It was this that startled them.

I was told to get on my horse,
the rest were told
to get in the wagons,
and then, with a man on each side,
whipping the teams,
we drove
furiously
towards Leavenworth.
We camped two miles
from Leavenworth
and about midnight we drove on
to the Rialto Ferry
on the Missouri River
opposite Weston.

There was a large bonfire
and many armed men there.
We were taken to Weston.
Then we were taken to Platte City.
There we were put in jail
on the 28th of January, 1859.

William Clarke Quantrell
would ride up
to the north ferry landing
at about nine in the morning
to meet the gang. Though the gang
called him Charley, Charley Hart,
he would just call them the gang.
Everyone in Lawrence, it is said,
called him Charley, Charley Hart,
though to everyone in Missouri
he was Charley Quantrell, even
in some cases Charles William
Quantrell.

      One day
a negro came out of the woods,
running, he was on a trail
that extended through the Delaware Reserve
and up to the north ferry landing
and he was running this day
young and a strong one
but he seemed weary
from this running and
the first man he saw
when he came out of these woods
at the north ferry landing
was Jake Herd who was
at work that day on the ferry boat.
The negro who came out of the woods
inquired of Jake

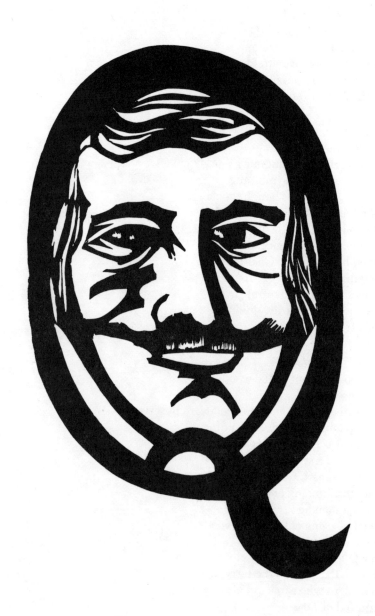

the way to the house of James H. Lane
saying he desired to go there.
Herd put him across
the river.
At the south ferry landing
were Baldwin and Q.
and they were loafing.
Herd told them
where the negro
who had just come running
out of the woods
so young and so strong
desired to go
and he told this negro
that they would take him
to the house of James Lane.
They said they would take him
to Lane's house,
certainly, they said,
they would take him to Lane's house.
Then they told him to
"come along".
The negro went along
with Q. and with Baldwin
and he answered their questions
freely.

He had escaped
from his owner, he said,
a widow named Gaines
who lived at
Platte City, Missouri.
He had come through Leavenworth
on the trail that extended
through the Delaware Reserve
running.

He had hoped
to get to Mr. Lane's house
where he would be safe.

They took him to McGee's.

That night
they tied this negro on a horse
and they took him to Westport,
where they stopped
in the woods near the town.
McGee rode on to Platte City
to arrange with the widow Gaines
for as large a reward
as could be wrung from her
for her slave's return.

She agreed to pay
five hundred dollars
for the return of this negro,
so young and so strong,
though the statutory reward was only
two hundred dollars.
McGee returned to Westport
and the next day
they took this negro to Platte City
and received the sum of
five hundred dollars,
all in new twenties
and from a Missouri bank.

The widow Gaines asked the slave
whose name was "Ike"
Gaines why he ran away.
He said
the keeper of the livery stable
told him to.

When Q.
and his friends
returned to Lawrence
they gave Jake Herd
one hundred dollars
of Mrs. Gaines' money.

(RICHARD P. GAINES b. in 1789; d.Sept. 6, 1854; m'd in Kentucky, Joanna Tinder, who survived him. He came to Platte City
in 1842, and purchased of J.V. Cockrell the frame hotel on the
southeast corner of what is now the public square. "He was a fat
and jolly landlord, and highly esteemed."—or so it says on page
187 of Paxton's Annals of Platte County, "the most complete history ever written of any county in the United States.")

Immediately after this incident
Q. disappeared: and we,
the readers of these annals,
lose sight of him.
It is only for two or three weeks
but it is two or three weeks
in his life.
Not even Jake Herd knew where he was,
though Herd has not yet told
the whole story
of what he knows:

During the summer of 1858, and for a year or two thereafter, I
was much of the time employed with the Baldwin boys operating
the old rope ferry across the Kansas river at this point, connecting
Lawrence with the Delaware Indian Reserve.

It was here at the ferry where I first met W.C. Quantrill, then
under the assumed name of Charles Hart. Hart claimed then to
be stopping with a son of Sarcoxie, a Delaware chief, a few miles
out on the reserve, and he frequently crossed the river with us going to and from Lawrence. At first Quantrill appeared to be rather

reticent, but after a time, crossing frequently as he did, he appeared to become more sociable, and often stopped and chatted with the boys, and after a time became more chummy, often spending a half hour or longer with us when we were not busy, practicing jumping with the boys, running short foot-races etc. He did not strike me as having any braggadocio or desire to make any display in any way. If he had any money, to amount to anything, no one knew it but himself. He did not appear to have any business or means of support, so far as I knew.

I don't think he had any very positive convictions on questions that were agitating the territory at that time; if he did, he certainly kept them to himself. One thing is certain, he was always willing to go into anything that turned up that had a dollar in it for Charley Hart.

During my acquaintance with Quantrill, he did not appear to be permanently located in any place, and would frequently leave without any warning to any one of us, and be gone for days, and sometimes weeks, and then turn up again as unexpectedly as he had departed.

The Loss of a Watch

A man from Kansas City
by the name of A. M. Winner,
or I. M. Winner,
says he has found
Q.'s watch.
Q. lost this watch
in an orchard
in Jackson county
during the war
more than thirty years ago.
After the watch was lost
in the orchard
the orchard was cut down,
the ground was plowed up
and the watch was found.
The finder of the watch
gave the watch to Mr. Winner,
to Mr. A. M. Winner
of Kansas City.
On the inside
of the back lid
of the case
is cut
with some sharp instrument
the name
"Charley Quantrell".
Q. called attention to the loss
of his watch
a few minutes after
he lost it
and he searched for the watch
for an hour or more.

He and his men
got their dinner that night
at the home of the man
who owned the orchard.
He was a prominent citizen
of Jackson County
and Q. requested him
to keep the matter in mind
and find the watch
if he could
which he did
but many years later.

A very interesting relic,
interesting from the
historical relations
of the man who once owned it,
was found on the farm of
Ink Hicklin
at Greenwood, near Lee's Summit,
a few weeks ago.
                    Oh? what's that?
It is the watch
once carried by
the famous renegade
Charles Quantrell
or Charley Hart,
and lost by him
on Mr. Hicklin's farm,
on Ink Hicklin's farm,
thirty-two years ago.
Quantrell and his band
were riding through the country
pursued by federal troops
at the time the watch was lost
and while hunting for the watch
Quantrell barely escaped
being captured.
                    Captured?! Quantrell?
The day after the watch was lost
Quantrell returned,
and with Mr. Ink Hicklin,
now living on the farm
upon which the watch was lost,
hunted for the watch
but failed to find it
and the watch lay there
for thirty-two years
until it was picked up by the man
who had helped its owner
look for the watch

when the owner's bones
had been dust
for many years
and his daring and heartless deeds
almost forgotten,
save for the blot
on the scroll of history
that is this.

                    That is what?
Why Quantrell should risk
being captured
to search for the watch
is a puzzling question.

                    It is
                    a puzzling question.
Certainly not
because of its
intrinsic value,
as the case is of brass,
at one time gold-plated.

                    Oh, well.
It is a hunting case,
and closed together well,
for the wheels are almost intact
after all the years
it has been exposed
to the elements
of Mr. Hicklin's farm,
of Ink Hicklin's farm.

                    Of whose?
Of Ink Hicklin's farm.
The name "Charles Quantrell"
is rudely cut
on the inner side
of the back cover
of the case
which is of brass,
and looks as if it had been done

with a pocket knife.
                    It does
                    look like
                    the work of
                    a knife.
That the watch is genuine,
Daniel Williams of Greenwood
will swear, he says,
for he saw Quantrell
cut the name on the case.
The watch belongs to
Jack Atkins,
a jeweler at Greenwood,
and it was when he
poured some acid on it,
to find what it was made of,
that the name was made legible.
                    And?
It was made of brass,
he found.
Mr. Atkins
sent the watch to
The Star
for inspection,
and it is undoubtedly genuine
says the Star.
                    Oh well,
                    then it is undoubtedly
                    genuine.
All the old settlers
in the neighborhood
where the watch was lost
on Ink Hicklin's farm
and found,
remember the circumstance
of Quantrell
losing his watch.
                    We do?

A Horse Race

But he returns, as always,
here he is again folks,
the star returns,
on a white horse,
of course,
White Stockings
is its name
because its white
feet strike
like stockings
the imagination
of the man who owns him:
Q.   Varmint Q.
now owns a race horse!
He plans to race
White Stockings
against the fastest horse
in Kansas.
Mulkey's Colt
is its name
because it is the colt
of William Mulkey
of Kansas City,
and a man with less
imagination
than the owner of
White Stockings.
Q. brings his race horse
White Stockings
to Westport (Kansas)
for the race.
Mr. Mulkey,
who brings Mulkey's Colt,

is supposed to be
        pretty good
with horses
or so everyone in Kansas says.
Q. is afraid
Mr. Mulkey won't bet
once he sees
White Stockings

so Q. puts on
a high-horned saddle
(what a dope
everybody says)
and he brings out
White Stockings
covered with mud!
(what a nag
they all say)
(*White* Stockings?
they all laugh)
and even Mr. Mulkey,
for once, is deceived.
He bets
one hundred and fifty dollars
on his own horse,
Mulkey's Colt,
to win (there being
no place or show bets
in a two-horse race).
White Stockings,
of course,
wins
       by a mile!
going away!
     no contest!
       hands down!
kuh-reist!
But nobody ever *really* loses,
come on folks:
Are there any other takers?
Q. asks. Q. stays in Westport
(Kansas) two more weeks
waiting for other takers.
There are no other takers.
What kind of fools
do you take us for,
they all say,

thinking, with this,
that Q. is a clever man
and thinking,
because of this,
that they have lost.

John Dean's Statement
in Reply to Interrogatories

"I met *Quantrell* as a *now* known spie and *assassin,* working in connection with *many others* for *reward of Earth.* He was a *sensitive, falsely polerized,* or polerized to *Evil*   Your description of him was fair but not positively correct or sharply drawn. He was some *taller* not less than 5–10   we have stood back to back & compared. I am 5–10½ strong and he less than ½ inch shorter. I never knew of his having a *picture* taken   his eyes were *uncommonly large* and *full.* he was quite *talkative* at times. Very *pleasant* as a studied rule, laughing & joking, not a loud boisterous laugh, but a rolling, rippling, quiet laugh. He was *acting* the spie in his connection with me and of course much of his seeming character was "put on.""

There was a reward of $5000 in gold on my life at that time, offered by Gov Clabe Jackson of Mo. for I was doing all I could then on the Under ground R.R. or freeing slaves. *he bought* his introduction to me through one professed rabid Anti slavery Lawyer by the name of Ingersoll at the time showing me letters & recommends from men then residing in Lykins Co. I will say to you that he *never* had *my* full confidence. I was always on my guard and many of his *plots* miscarried in consequence. What time he was spending around Lawrence was in *one* way active he was very temperate as I now remember, but did at last, or about 1861 begin to have his little times of a drink or two, did not use tobacco in any way as I remember, but was given to the worship of women somewhat. his time was spent much with those lawless and reckless neer do *wells* that abound in such times and places. When asked *why* he *did* associate with such characters, he claimed to be spieing *their* plans, with the intention of doing good and was often telling of some scheme of theirs to kidnap colored people to sell again, and in the carrying out of one of these plots he got himself and his pro-slavery friends in-

dicted by the Grand jury of Lawrence and I escaped the snair
that was laid in the plot."

Allen Pinks
was a light colored mulatto
of about twenty years of age
born at Pittsburg in Pennsylvania
his grandmother being a German woman
as he informed me

Allen Pinks
had been cook and head waiter
on board of steamboats
on the Mississippi and Missouri Rivers
and had last been paid off
at St Joseph Missouri

From there he started for
Leavenworth
walking down the Missouri bank
of the river
with a white man
who had been on the steamboat with him

At the Rialto Ferry Allen Pinks
was stopped by the Ferryman
on suspicion of being a fugitive slave
and lodged in Weston calaboose
till he was transferred to
Platte city jail

He had left his free papers
with a free colored wagon-builder
at Independence Missouri
because he thought they were wearing out

As it was for the interest of those concerned

in detaining him
that he should not prove himself free
he could get no one to send to
Independence
though only thirty miles distant
and ascertain whether his assertion
were true or were false

To finish Pinks' story
I Doctor John Doy will state
that after my rescue
from the hands of those Missourians
expecting an attempt to recapture me
I was fortified at Mr Stearns' brick block
in the center of Lawrence
for nearly a month

One morning about five o'clock
I was called by Mr. Stearns
who informed me that a rough-looking man
who said he was from Platte City
was asking for Mr Doy at the front door

I looked out from my upper window
and whom should I see but
Allen Pinks

Allen Pinks
was nearly naked
having nothing on but shirt and trowsers
and those almost torn to pieces
When let in
Allen Pinks accounted for
his dilapidated appearance
by saying that he had travelled a bee line
from Platte City
and having been in somewhat of a hurry
had not paid sufficient respect
to the thorns and briers he met with

He had swum the Missouri River
above Leavenworth
and come into Lawrence
through the Delaware Reserve
begged a passage over Kaw River
and finally arrived in safety
at the city of refuge
Lawrence

We bound up and healed
his cut legs and feet
and sent to Pittsburg Pennsylvania
for his free papers

They reached us 14th September 1859
and were supported by the affidavits
of Mr William McArthur and Dr F G Gallagher
of Pittsburg
who had known Allen Pinks from his birth

When they came I said to him
"Pinks I've got something for you"

"What is it Doctor John Doy" he said

"Your free papers" I said

"Oh" he said

"You don't seem to care much" I said

"Why should I Doctor John Doy" he said
"What good will they do me?
Haven't we seen plenty of free papers
torn up and burnt
in Platte City jail" he said

Allen Pinks
is now employed in the Johnson House
in Lawrence
is considered one of the best
and steadiest hands there
but says he had had sufficient experience
of the blessings of freedom
for colored men in this Union
especially in the state of Missouri

That state did indeed keep him
for three months without any charge
for rent or board
but as
if he had stayed one month more

he would have been sold at the auction block
like a beast
he prefers not to try her hospitality again

> One day Allen Pinks
> turned
> on his own people.
> This was because
> Quantrell
> was using Allen Pinks
> as a decoy
> to run free negroes
> and fugitive slaves
> into the hands of Jake Herd
> for kidnapping.
> At the same time,
> Quantrell also worked for
> the underground railroad people.
> Quantrell would kidnap
> a slave one day
> out of slavery
> and deliver him to
> the underground railroad people.
> Then he would kidnap
> the same slave
> back again from
> the underground railroad people
> and sell him back the next day
> into slavery.
> In this way
> Quantrell made
> much the best
> of both sides.
> When
> the underground railroad people
> heard
> Allen Pinks
> had turned

on his own people,
they decided he must be
put to death.
So they told their man
Quantrell
to kill Allen Pinks.
But Quantrell decided
it would be wasteful
to kill Allen Pinks
when he could just as easily
sell him back again
into slavery
so Quantrell got his friend
Bob Wilson
to ask Allen Pinks
who at that time was working
in a barber shop
in Lawrence
to come over to
Bob Wilson's house
to set his wife's hair
pretending that she was sick
and could not set her own hair.
Allen Pinks
didn't want to go
because he knew
something was up
but he went anyway
and when he got to the house
and saw two kidnappers
coming at him
he ran out of the house
and into the woods
and though the kidnappers
chased after him
he got away.
John Dean
who was one of the

underground railroad people
was much upset
when he heard that
Quantrell
had not killed Allen Pinks
so John Dean himself
took a small rifle
and when he saw Allen Pinks
taking a drink
from the public well
in the center of Lawrence
he shot him
in the back of the head
with his rifle.
But the thickness of the skull
on Allen Pinks
saved his life
because the rifle-ball
glanced off the skull
and ran around just under the skin
and lodged in his forehead.

John Dean afterwards
turned himself in
and was put in jail in Lawrence
for attempted murder.

Allen Pinks
was finally shot
by an enraged mob of his own people
at Leavenworth, Kansas.

William Clarke Quantrell,
as usual, got away.

The Morgan Walker Raid

And there were these good men: there was
Charles Ball of Salem, Ohio,
who moved to Iowa
to the Springdale Settlement
in 1852.
There was Chalkley T. Lipsey,
a Quaker, born in Ohio,
who went to Pike's Peak to dig
for gold in 1860.
But he didn't find any,
and he walked back to Pardee,
Atchison County, famished,
frozen, but ready for the raid
though he had never been to Missouri before,
on a raid, or otherwise.
There was Edwin S. Morrison
who was from Buffalo when the family moved
to the Springdale Settlement
in 1853.
And there was Albert Southwick, from Ohio,
a cousin of Edwin Morrison,
and Ransom L. Harris,
from Vermont, who came to Kansas
in 1859
he says especially for the purpose
of liberating slaves
on the underground railroad.
And these good men
belonged to a secret lodge
in the Springdale Settlement
(which was Quaker) which John Brown,
himself, used to visit,
when he stationed his men there

in 1858.
And the secret of this Quaker lodge was
that these good men
ran the Missouri line
on an underground railroad.

These then were the men
who went with Quantrell
on the Morgan Walker Raid.

But how did Quantrell
get in with such men
to go on such a raid?
It was on the day after the Sheriff,
Sam Walker, tried
to arrest Quantrell,
when Quantrell ran
into John Dean's shop,
when Quantrell was hiding,
three miles northwest
of Lawrence, Kansas, in the woods,
when these five abolitionists
came riding by,
and with the help of John Dean,
who himself was a known abolitionist,
that Quantrell wangled
a ride to Missouri for the raid.

The plan was put forth
by three black Cherokee
refugee slaves
at the Springdale Settlement,
and it was for the five abolitionists
of this good Quaker settlement
to go into the Cherokee nation
and bring out the others,
the relatives of these three
black Cherokee refugee

slaves, but when they got to
Osawatomie,
and John Dean told
Captain Ely Snyder
what the plan was,
he said no, he did not
think it would work, no,
that he knew very well
this man Quantrell,
that he did not trust him
at all, so the abolitionists
decided to have nothing more
to do with Quantrell.
The invasion of the Cherokee nation
was abandoned. Quantrell
began to plan then
the Morgan Walker Raid,
in which he saw an opportunity
to kidnap three
black refugee slaves
and sell them to Missouri for ransom,
and he argued shrewdly so,
with these three men
to go to Missouri with him,
to Morgan Walker's house,
where they could induce the slaves there
to leave in a body and fight.
Q. finally convinced
all these good men
to go along with him
on the Morgan Walker Raid.

OSAWATOMIE, FEB. 14, 1883

in the year 1860 some time in the month of Dec Late one Evening
10 men and a two horses wageon with one man the oner of the
Team wich would make 11 men Stopt at my house in Osawatomie
ask me to Stay all Night I Told them that my House was Small

92

that I could not accomodate them   thay said thay must Stay if
thay had to Stay in the barn   they wair all Strangers to me at
that time and I thought that thay might not be on Eny good as
thay was one Thousand dollars Reward for me then in Masurie
I had a emty house a short distance from mine and give them the
key and told them to go in that house which thay did thair was
7 white men and 3 black men besides the teamster wich went
away the next morning   the ten Stayed in the house but I seen
thay had Som Object in Vew but did not tell me what it was for
Som days when thay told me that thay started from Larrance with
the intention of going toe the Cherekee Nation to bring out Some
Slaves and wanted me to take my team and wageon and go with
them as thair Captain I decline and told them it was in the cold
winter and it wold take a big sum of Money to Accomplish eny
thing and I found out that thay had Little Money So I perswaded
them that thay had better let the Job out at present they then
perposed that thay wold cut me Some wood thay all went to wurk
but Quantrill and he made his hedquarters at the Post Office   it
was then proslavery post office and the plan of the rade on Walker
was in my nowing got up in the Post Office at Osawatomie and
had it not been for myself perswadeing the 9 men Quantrill wold
have got all the party in the same boat as he did the three that he
perswaded to go with him   I went to the Timber wair theas wair
at work and got them all together and told them that I knew that
Quantrill wold get them in troble if thay did go with him   John
M. Dean, Albert Southwork and John Jones, William Thomson
John Thomson and John Martin   the three last names are the
names of the three black men   thay wair Cherekeys fugitives
thay wair Intelligent black men and So wair all of the white men
the Six names that I have mentioned took my Advice and did not
go with Quantrill to Walkers but the other three got very Indig-
nant at me for thinking that Quantrell wold by Gilty of geting
them in troble   the name of the three that wair killd at Walkers
ones name was Charles Ball. the others Last names I dont remember   the thair anechiates wair Charles and Edwent and the three
went from my House on the morning thay started for Walkers and

Quantrell started from the Post Office I walked with them a short distance and bid them good by and told them that I did not expect to ever see them again thay went on and met with thair fate it may be that I can get thair names in future but I will say that John M. Dean was not at Walkers nun but Quantrell and the 3 that I have mentioned

Morgan Walker was a Kentuckian,
who settled near Blue Springs,
Jackson County, Missouri,
in 1834.
A man of affairs, he owned
two thousand acres,
a house with nine rooms,
five down and four
up, thirty slaves,
more than a hundred horses,
and a large sum of gold,
which he kept, hidden, in his house.

Quantrell, and his men,
camped near the house,
several days prior
to the day they moved on the house.
They talked with the slaves and got
satisfactory responses beforehand.
The attack was made on the night
after they got to the house.
Morgan Walker rode
to Independence that day,
and he passed Quantrell
on the road with the men near his house.
Quantrell asked
Morgan Walker the way
to his house and Walker replied
that he was Morgan Walker.

Quantrell knew
Walker well even
if Walker did not know
Quantrell, so
he asked Walker, shrewdly,
if his sons were home. They were.

When they were a mile from the house, they camped,
in a thicket. Quantrell
went on to the house of Andrew
Walker, son of Morgan
Walker, a quarter mile
from the house of Morgan Walker.
He told Andrew Walker
that some men were coming from Kansas
that night, to rob his father,
Morgan Walker, that they were waiting
a mile from his house, that he,
Quantrell, was sent
to look things over.
He told Walker everything.
He told him to do whatever
he thought would be proper. And
it was agreed that Quantrell
should lead his men to the house,
aid in killing them, and remain
with Walker, with Andrew Walker.
Andrew Walker informed
four neighbors, who came,
arming themselves with double-
barreled shotguns.
On the porch near the little room
at the north end of the house
Mrs. Walker had her loom.
Andrew put three men
in the little room, while he
and the other men hid
behind the loom itself.
It was agreed that Quantrell
and his men should go into the house
to talk with Morgan Walker
about taking away his slaves
and that Quantrell should remain
in the house, and when the others went out
to gather up the slaves,

they were to be fired on while still
on the porch in the light from the door.

Morgan Walker came home,
from Independence, ten
minutes before the men
arrived with Quantrell.
It was ten minutes to seven.
He was immediately told everything.
Quantrell and his men
arrived at seven o'clock.
Morrison was left on the porch.
Dean was stationed in the yard.
Quantrell wanted
everyone to go into the house,
but only he, Lipsey, and Ball
agreed to go into the house.
It was Charles Ball who said
they had come to take the slaves,
that they would also take his horses,
and that they would take the gold in his house.
Walker asked Ball
if he had talked with his slaves and was told
that the slaves had been consulted.
Walker told him to go then
and take the slaves to Kansas
but that if any of the slaves objected
to going to Kansas for freedom
that they were to be left at home.
Quantrell told
Ball to go out and
gather up the slaves,
and that he would remain in the house
to take care of the old folks.
Quantrell remained
with Morgan Walker and the family
and Ball and Lipsey went out
onto the porch into the light from the door.

Morrison fell dead.
Lipsey fell wounded.
Ball leaped from the porch
and fired his pistol at random.
Ball returned to Lipsey
to take him, wounded, to the wagon,
but Dean had been wounded too
and had taken the wagon and rode out
to Lawrence, the city of refuge.
Southwick ran after the wagon.

(Let it be added, however, that
Major John Edwards,
who says he got his information
about this incident
from Frank and Jesse James,
who once rode with Quantrell,
tells it this way:

The night was dark. It had rained a little during the day, and the most of the light of the stars had been put out by the clouds, when Quantrell arranged his men for the dangerous venture. They were to proceed first to the house, gain possession of it, capture the male members of the family, put them under guard, assemble the negroes, bid them hitch up all the wagons and teams possible, and then make a rapid gallop for Kansas.

Fifty yards from the main gate the eight men dismounted and fastened their horses. Arms were looked to, and the stealthy march to the house began. Quantrell led. He was very cool, and seemed to see everything. The balance of the marauders had their revolvers in their hands; his were in his belt. Not a dog barked. If any there had been aught save city bred, this, together with the ominous silence, would have demanded a reconnaisance. None heeded the surroundings, however, and Quantrell knocked loudly and boldly at the oaken panels of Morgan Walker's door. No answer. He knocked again and stood perceptibly to one side. Suddenly, and as though it had neither bolts nor bars, locks nor hinges, the door flared open and Quantrell leaped into the hall with a bound like a red deer. 'Twas best so. A livid sheet of flame burst out from the darkness where he had disappeared—as though an explosion had happened there—followed by another as the second barrels of the guns were discharged, and the tragedy was over. Six fell where they stood, riddled with buck-shot. One staggered to the garden, bleeding fearfully, and died there. The seventh, hard hit and unable to mount his horse, dragged his crippled limbs to a patch of timber and waited for the dawn. They tracked him by his blood upon the leaves and found him early. Would he surrender? No! Another volley, and the last Liberator was liberated. Walker and his two sons, assisted by three of his stalwart and obliging neighbors, had done a clean night's work and a righteous one. Those who had taken the sword had perished by it.

A Lie / A Dream / A History

Because he said he was born
in Hagerstown, Maryland
he was not born there,
in 1836, as he said he was,
though he lived there, or said he did,
until he was 16, but it was a lie,
he did not live there
a devoted son, as he said he was,
who helped his widowed mother
and in his 16th year said
he was taken to Cleveland, Ohio
by an old friend of the family,
there given an excellent English education.
Me and my older brother, he said,
and a negro a wagon and a team,
he said, started for Pike's Peak
and arrived at Lawrence, Kansas.
We stopped to make some purchases, he said,
and left in the afternoon.
We camped near the Kaw River, he said,
where during the night we were attacked
by a group called Montgomery's band.
My brother was killed, he said,
and I was wounded, left for dead,
the negro the wagon and the team
were all appropriated.
After keeping vigil for 24 hours
amidst hundreds of coyotes
and famished for water, he said,
I crawled to the Kaw River
and managed to quench my thirst,
after which I espied a canoe
on the opposite bank

and an Indian
soon after approached the canoe,
to whom I halloed,
Hello, Halloo, I said,
asking him to come over,
and he did, he came over,
and he heard my story
and he buried my brother
after he came over, he said.
He and his wife, he said,
nursed me back to health.
He was a Shawnee Indian and
his name was Golightly Spiebuck.
Soon after I was nursed back to health
by him and his wife, I sought out
this group called Montgomery's band,
and I joined Montgomery's band.
My name was Charley Hart, he said.
I then obtained in a systematic way
the names of all the men
who took part killing my brother.
I joined the group called Montgomery's band
for the purpose of revenge, he said,
managing to get one at a time
away from the camp,
and I never let one get back alive,
until, when the war came on,
only two were left.
       This is most of what he said
to the Missourians.

The man I knew as W.C. Quantrill always said he was born and
raised in Hagerstown, Md. When he became such a noted rebel
partisan chieftain his mother had to leave home went to Virginia
was there when he was wounded and died in Louisville, Kentucky, he wrote to her all the time he was in the state he told me a
few days before he was wounded about his relatives said he had

three brothers one was killed in Kansas when they were on their way to Colorado while they were in camp one night the Jayhawkers as they were afterwards called came on them in the night killed his brother shot him breaking his leg left him for dead took their outfit and negro man they had and left his second brother killed fiting under the gallant Stone Wall Jackson in Virginia his other brother a lad twelve years old was a cripple at home with his Mother and Sister about eighteen years of age. you say he was born at Canal Dover Ohio is why I think there must have been two men of the same name as Thompson Quantrill so I cannot give any information concerning the one you speak of the one I knew was true to the cause for which he fought and a son that any Mother might be proud off as to the questions you ask I could never think of writing not being much of a hand at letter writing as you see when you read this I know brave deeds and hair bredth escapes of him and his brave company but dates I cannot remember he was a true Catholic this Thompson said they were all Presbyterians the Priest name was Powers but I have heard that he died about a year ago. Capt. Quantrill was buried in the Catholic grave yard between Louisville and Portland, Ky. I have his photograph but I can not send it from the fact it is not at home at present tis a good likeness of him.

—OLIVIA D. COOPER

      If there were
two hundred men with the same name
it would not be the same as this one man
with two hundred names,
even if they all lived in the same state
and that state were, well, Kansas!
and even if every one of their two hundred stories
made sense.
           Q.,
you was stealing oxen from Beeson then,
remember? and blankets and pistols
from Torrey. You was never
an innocent injured Maryland boy

in the cabin of a Shawnee
named Golightly Spiebuck.
Go on! You was gambling then,
remember? and that, at least,
was in your favor.

A day or two after, one of Walkers slaves found the other two in
the woods, while looking up a missing horse, and found the horse
tied with them. Ball was seemingly "all right" and had a small
camp fire, was making a poultace of bark for Harry, who was
dying of his wounds The slave left the horse with them and prom-
ised not to betray them, but did immediately go and tell Walker,
who summoned his "army" and guided by the negro, surrounded
the "camp." when Ball saw them approaching he at once knew
that he was "lost" and singling out Quantrell who stood beside
Walker, dared him to come near enough to give him a fair chance.
Ball stood over his dying comrade and shook his pistol at the at-
tacking party Walker himself, being armed with a long range
rifle, shot Ball in the forehead and killed him instantly. When
Ball fell, Quantrell ran up, looked at Harry and Ball, put his revolver into Harrys mouth and fired, and there was no one of the
party to tell Walker any different story than Quantrells.

—JOHN DEAN

          As if,
and whatever you say, Q.,
the truth is
there are not even two
of your many persons here,
the truth is this dream
you are making of what you think is
your history, that is your history,
of what you cannot get out of your head,
of what you will not let out of your mouth.

The sheriff came and took Quantrill to Independence and put him in jail. I went with him to that place and got the Sheriff to let him out that night. I took him to the Hotel and we slept in the same room. A great many people were in town the next day and the excitement ran very high. In the afternoon I thought it time to start home and went to the stable to get my horse. When I arrived on the public square, I found a great crowd gathered about. I rode up to them to see what it meant and learned that they were going to hang Quantrill. I told them they must not do it; but some of them seemed inclined to be stubborn about it. I told them if they did, they would do it over my dead body and they gave it up. I then went with Quantrill and bought him a suit of clothes of which he was badly in need and we went home. The next day my father gave him a horse, bridle and saddle and $50.00 in money with the understanding that he was to leave, as it was thought best. He left for Kansas; but told me he would be back in a few days and he was. He made two or three trips into Kansas. He was caught once and put in jail at Aubrey, I think.

—ANDREW J. WALKER

       Thus,
on the 25th of March, 1861,
Varmint Q. rode back to Staunton, Kansas,
and he rode back singing, but
what he sang was the music of a dream he had,
called simply,

            A DREAM I HAD
Almost as an afterthought
the winds beat their tension into your dream,
into it, out of it, and then you remember,
after the winds remind you, that is,
then you can remember,
you are not the outlaw but
the dream of an outlaw, and
later on you will be the wind itself
and then perhaps yourself an afterthought

you will know about the constancy of names
in such province and states of your mind

An unimposing act of will—
the first man to open his mouth
and thus lose illusion
had to be an Adam of inconstancy:
Adam it was when once that great and foolish wind
swept through his yard,
uprooting everything,
leaving hundreds homeless,
yet this wind was not a hurricane,
and consequently had no name

It was only as an afterthought
that Adam thought of his possessions—
all lemons, and the mayberry bush,
nasturtiums and grizzlies and
you name it

Was it ever anything more
than an act of loudness?   Yes!
Adam shouted and an Earth woke up
or the Earth shook and Adam woke up
or somebody heard the wind come in
and said so   and was it you?   No!

When Captain Elias Snyder heard
who it was was coming
back to Kansas, when he heard
that is, that it was Quantrill
who was coming back to Kansas,
he immediately armed his men,
he armed his men
and arrested Varmint Q.

Erly in the spring of 61 I do not now remember the day of the
month or the month at this time but can get the date of the time
to the day   Late in the evening Squire Hauser sent me a message

that Quantrill was at Bennings I got 5 men to go with me and
captive the outlaw and bring him to Justice with a inch roap
when we came near to Bennings I left the party and in the woods
and went to Hausers House and Hauser advised me to make the
arest under the shade of Law as I did not think best but Mr.
Hauser was at the time Justice of the Peace and I gave way to his
Plan and he apointed me Constable and then reconsidered it and
thought best to give the papers in the Hand of the Constable
which was Jurd said that Jurd would be all right Jurd proved
to be a friend to Quantrell and spoiled the hole Bisness he Jurd
told me that he would go in and being acquainted with Benings
that he had warrant for Quantrell to have him run out at the back
door and then we could get him but Jurd did not do that. he told
Quantrell that I had a posse of men out side and for him not to go
out or I would get him so Jurd made me fals prommas and kept
me waiting until almost daylight when I hured the thing up by
bursting open the door and stept in the house Quantrell was
standing in the middle door with a Revolver in each hand Quantrell attempted to rais and bring them to range on me when I
spoke to him and said bill drop them revolvers or I will kill you
I had my Revolver in range of the place wair he Lived he Obaid
quick I then told him to hand them Revolvers to Jurd which he
did he then was taken to Squire Hausers office and Jurd and
Bening sent to Paola for Millar and White and Potter theas three
Proslaves came and waved examination and he would go to Jail
So the Constable Jurd took him to Jail Shortly after that I got a
order from Sheriff and he depetized me and ordered me to bring
Wm Quantrell to Larrance and turn him over to the athorities of
Douglis Co I shoed my papers to H.H.Williams and my demand
he would have to give up the Prisner He said he could not go to
Paola for 2 hours but would send his depety wich was Jim Cree
to see that Quantrell was not taken out of Jail before we got over
and Cree said that Williams told him to go to White and tell
White that Snyder had a order to take him Quantrill to Larance
and when Williams and Myself came in paola Quantrell was Left
out of Jail and on the horse that Walker giv Him for his Sirvis of
Geting Some of the Kansas Abilishens kild.

—CAPTAIN ELY SNYDER

107

Cost.	
docket	$.10
oath	.10
warrant	.50
3 papers	.30
trying	.75
order	.35
mittim.	.35
docket	.25

	$2.70

State of Kansas
Against Quantrill ⎬ Criminal Action

Eli Snyder for State.
Before me, Samuel H. Houser a Justice
of the Peace for said Lykins County,
personally came Eli Snyder who being
duly sworn according to law says there
was a warrant issued to Constable
E.B. Jurd on 26th day of March, 1861.
Warrant served on prisoner in custody.

E.B. JURD CONST.

From sleep, he said,
the strong awake,
the weak escape, but
everyone seems
to come out of it,
it is the same
act, a sad fact,
not like
death which is
only a
pleasant lesson

I came home on a short furlow leaving my Horse at Home I went
to Staunton telling my wife I would be back in one or 2 hours. I
carried my Revolver with me as I walked up to the only Store in
the town Quantrell and a man by the name of Jurd a Constable
was standing about 30 feet from the Store House I shook Hands
with them I saw five men Walking very fast coming in our direction about 20 yards off they Had Sharps Rifles slung over their
shoulders Mr Jurd said to me I depotize you to Protect Quantrell
from those men I knew 2 of them One of them was Elias Snyder
the other was called Buckskin as they came near one of them
drew his gun to shoot Quantrell I knocked the gun up and drew
my Revolver and said Whats up Quantrell said they are going
to kill me I said what for he said he did not know Quantrell
was very Pale and Excited I said if there is any shooting I would
take a Hand in it and ordered Quantrell to go into the Store
thoes men had their guns cocked and trying to get a shot at him
I kept my Pistol Presented in their direction saying I would shoot
the man that fired the first shot. When Quantrell got in the store
I held the door there was a ladder standing in the center of the
Floor reaching to the Sealing I ordered Quantrell to enter a square
Hole in cealing When he was up I walked in and Started up the
Ladder saying that the first man that stuck his head above the
trap door I would kill there was one bed up there I found Quan-
trell sitting on it They ordered me to come down or they would
shoot through the floor but they did not know just where we were

then they said they would burn the house the Store Keeper to
save his Building tried to get us to come down Quantrell said to
me to give him my pistol and for me to go down and he would sell
his life to the best advantage I told him he was my prisoner and
that I would turn him over to the Sheriff I had told Jurd to send
some one after the Sheriff and Possey to Paola He sent a man by
the name of John Billings on Quantrells Horse it was 10 miles in
less than three hours the Sheriff came with 4 good men I turned
Quantrell over to them next day they send a Man out to my Place
for me to come to Paola I went in they wanted to know why I
had Quantrell under arest I was in the Jail talking with Quantrell
and the Sheriff I stated that I had taken him to save his life. In
less than 20 minutes he was out and gone. He went straight for
Missouri and took the Bush.

—REV. ROBERT SHEARER

                    Again!
he put his thumb to his nose,
this man, this Varmint Q.,
a gesture of . . . what? of will?
and then—
and then   perhaps as an afterthought
leaning back in the saddle
he patted himself!   on the ass!
a vulgar gesture!
(but a dream!)
an insult to everyone!
and then—and then
he put spurs to his horse,
he opened his mouth—EIYEE!
and bade farewell to Kansas

The Guerilla

Morgan Walker had a daughter,
whose name was Anna,
but they called her Nannie, Walker.
Nannie Walker married a doctor,
whose name was Slaughter,
so her name became
Anna Walker Slaughter.
They lived with another doctor,
whose name has never been known.
One winter it was very cold,
and since there was no fireplace
in the room of this other doctor
Nannie Walker made him a bed on the floor
in the room of herself and Doctor Slaughter
where there was a fireplace
where this other doctor could sleep.
One night Doctor Slaughter woke up
to find his wife getting back into bed.
He said nothing
but the next night he pretended to sleep
when his wife got up out of his bed
and got into bed with this other doctor.
She stayed there a long time.
Doctor Slaughter got up
and tried to kill this other doctor
but he escaped and so Doctor Slaughter
got a divorce from his wife
who returned to her father,
whose name was Morgan Walker.

This was a short time
before the raid on Morgan Walker's house.
And when Quantrill led the raid
on Morgan Walker's house
he fell in love with Morgan Walker's daughter.

(Yes,
love comes to Varmint Q. too
in the form of Anna Nannie Walker Slaughter,
in the form of A. Slaughter,
as all else, a tale, a sign,
that love comes to Varmint Q. at all
is a sign, and he, at heart,
a reader of signs, read this one
and acted upon it.)

112

After the raid on Morgan Walker's house
Q. returned to his life with the Indians
and though he liked his life with the Indians
because he liked, best of all, scalping the dead,
he soon gave this up and joined General Price
who was marching his troops to Missouri
because it was in Missouri
that he could see Morgan Walker's daughter.
Still, he kept up the life of an Indian.
He wore a black feather in his hair
when he went into battle with General Price.
Q. went into battle only a few times
with General Price and soon gave this up
and returned to Jackson County.
When he returned to Jackson County
he told Morgan Walker's son,
whose name was Andrew Walker
that some soldiers from Kansas
were robbing citizens again
on the farm of Strawder Stone.
They raised eleven men
and rode to Strawder Stone's
where one of the soldiers had just hit Mrs. Stone
on the head with a pistol.
Q. and his men shot this man
and wounded two others.
And the soldier killed by Quantrill
on Strawder Stone's farm
was the first Federal soldier killed
in Jackson County, Missouri
                                in the Civil War.
                    So,
it took this soldier's death
to start this
                    civil war:
with a bullet from Q.'s gun
war begins, as earlier,

with a smile, lopsided on his face,
love began.
                    If you would be the god of war
                    come forward.
                    If you would be the goddess,
                    love, come forward.
                    William Clarke Quantrell
                    and Anna Nannie Walker Slaughter
                    come forward.
But a man who would scalp the dead,
a woman who would share her bed
                    with doctors!
                    (because they too were expert
                    with a knife?)
Let us now pronounce them man and wife!
No, they do not marry.
She later marries Joe Vaughan.
Q. never marries at all.
There's a war on, he says.

And five new men
in Aubry, Kansas,
went out one evening
in search of honey,
or that is what they said
they were doing,
and that was all
they were doing,
they went out as they said
to gather honey,
they were such good men,
they told their wives
they would be back early,
we will be back early, they said,
we are only going out
in search of honey,
and it was the truth.
But Q. and his men

met
these five new Kansas men
who went out
that lovely evening
so sweetly,
so innocent, it would seem,
in their search for nothing but honey,
and he shot them,
Q. shot all five of these good men,
whose names were
Greenbury Trekle,
Mr. Whitaker,
Washington Tullis,
Ellis Cody, and
John Cody.

My first acquaintance with William C. Quantrell was in the
winter of 1858 & 1859—he was then teaching school near Stanton
in Miami County & I was Superintendent—I visited his school, &
put up, at his boarding house—I found him an interesting well ed-
ucated man—we slept together & talked until after 2 P.M. The
next thing I heard of him he had turned Abolitionist & was acting
as a conductor on the under ground Railroad & assisting Negroes
from Missouri to Canada—But he was not prompted by con-
science, or pure unadulterated religion—as he was never known to
assist any Negro unless the Negro first assisted him to steal a horse
or mule—The stock was Quantrells & the Negro passed North
through Iowa to Canada . . . And my next interview with Quantrell was on the 7th of March, 1862 I stopped for the night at
Aubrey in Johnson county, Kan—Not anticipating any trouble—
But at daylight I was awoke by the cry—The cut throats are coming—But before I could dress the house was surrounded and they
were yelling & screaming & swearing like Devils—and five men
who were in the lower rooms started to run across the fields But
were soon overtaken and butchered there were five of us upstairs
(all travelers) & about thirty of them were riddling the house with
bullets while these men were being butchered in the field & I was

carelessly looking out at the window up stairs & Quantrell saw me
through the window & gave me a dip—he made a good shot—(or
as he afterwards expressed it, a dam'd good shot)   I was struck in
the center of the forehead where the brains of most men are supposed to be located—I fell & was supposed to be dead—the others
then went down stairs & surrendered & in a few moments Quantrell & two others of the gads hill Band Came up stairs—each had
a revolver in his hand—with the hammer raised   They were trem-
bling like criminals & Swearing like Devils & to give an idea of
their interesting language—I will give a few detached sentences—I
was lieing on a mattress at the head of the stairs & they had been
told by the prisoners that there was only one man up stairs & he
was probably dead—So Quantrell and two others started upstairs
& as soon as they got within about four feet of me they all pointed
their revolvers at my head, with their fingers on the trigger—at last
one of them balled out—If you have any Money God damn you
give it to me in a minute or I'll blow you to Hell and as I had no
hankering after that place—I passed over the checks—(or in other
words) I handed him $250.00   they then passed on & searched the
rooms & I heard one of them say, that he had found a pocket book
& that it was a damned fat one—They then ordered me downstairs
& said that I was not dead by a damned sight—I then crawled
downstairs & was helped into a chair & in a few minutes Quantrell came down stairs & then recognized me & then got a cloth &
some water & washed my face & said he did it himself & was
damned sorry for it—as I was one of the Kansas men he did not
want to hurt—I then told him of my team & about fifty dollars
worth of groceries that were there in the house   he said that he
was glad that I had told him, as he was sorry for what he had already done & said that not one thing more of mine should be
touched & soon after I fainted away & lay on the frozen ground
about four hours senseless & motionless & to all appearances dead
& all who saw me pronounced me dead. I was really supposed to
be dead by all who saw me & if any of my Ohio friends are anxious
to see my likeness & the bullet and portions of my skull bones all
they have to do is to call at the army Medicinal Museum in Washington City—D.C. I am a native Buckeye—was born and raised in
Green County, Ohio—But the only redeeming traits I ever saw in
Quantrell was that he showed by his kindness to me, after I was

wounded that he was not entirely a Demon—But history will re-
cord him a desperately bad man—a highway robber, of the dark-
est shade & a desperate leader of a set of the most desperate
Demons that ever disgraced the name of man—infinitely worse
than he was. None of them with bravery enough to meet an enemy
—But they took every advantage of the surroundings—by treach-
ery to drench the earth with blood & carnage—

—ABRAHAM ELLIS

A large depression
size of a baby's fist
in his forehead,
everyone would call this man
Bullet-hole Ellis
because of this wound
from Q.'s pistol.
Q. the giver of ever-lasting first names.

Special Orders,
    No. 47.

HEADQRS. DISTRICT OF
CENTRAL MISSOURI

JEFFERSON CITY, MO.,
APRIL 21, 1862

I. It is represented on reliable authority at these headquarters
that bands of Jayhawkers, guerillas, marauders, murderers and
every species of outlaw are infesting to an alarming extent all the
southwestern portion of Jackson county, and that persons of in-
fluence and wealth in these vicinities are knowingly harboring and
thus encouraging (if not more culpably connected with) these
bands of desperadoes. A prairie known as "The Doctor Lee
Prairie", its borders and surroundings, are mentioned as the
haunts of these outlaws and the farmers generally in these neigh-
borhoods are said to be knowing to and encouraging the lawless
acts of these guerillas, etc., as mentioned above. Murders and rob-
beries have been committed; Union men threatened and driven
from their homes; the U.S. mails have been stopped; farmers have
been prohibited planting by the proclamation of a well-known
and desperate leader of these outlaws by the name of Quantrill,
and the whole country designated reduced to a state of anarchy.
This state of things must be terminated and the guilty punished.
All those found in arms and open opposition to the laws and legiti-
mate authorities, who are known familiarly as guerillas, jayhawkers, murderers, marauders, and horse-thieves, will be shot down
by the military on the spot when found perpetrating their foul

acts. All who have knowingly harbored and encouraged these outlaws in their lawless deeds will be arrested and tried by a military commission for their offenses, and those who have harbored and fed such miscreants as guerillas etc., but against whom clear proof cannot be obtained and who profess ignorance of having done these wrongs will be put under heavy bonds and security for their future good conduct or confined until they give such bonds etc.

II.   In order to correct the evils mentioned in the preceding paragraph and insure the passage of the mails regularly, Lieut. E.B. Brown, Seventh Missouri Volunteers, commanding the counties of Jackson and Cass will station one company of cavalry about five miles north of Pleasant Hill on the southern and one company on the northern border of the "Doctor Lee Prairie" to punish these guerillas and escort the mail in safety whenever necessary.

III.   Major Carley, commanding post at Warrensburg, will send one company First Iowa Cavalry to proceed to Pleasant Hill and escort the mail now there through to Independence, when it will return again to its present post.

By order of Brig. Gen. James Totten, commanding district.

—Lucien J. Barnes,
Captain and Assistant
Adjutant-General

From this 15th day of August, 1862,
I, William Clarke Quantrill,
alias Charley Hart,
Alias Varmint Q.,
alias anything-you-want,
shall be known as Captain Quantrill.
I am a captain, I am,
a captain, you will address me as
your captain, not as an outlaw,
you are soldiers, you have at last
found a war, the confederacy
is now responsible for you,
the enemy cannot now hang you,

the confederacy now has to pay you,
I am a captain,
you are my troops,
I am Captain Quantrill,
a captain, your captain,
o I am a captain
of this grand army you are.

I saw no more of him until September, 1862—when he sacked Olathe. He had with him at that time 220 men. Quantrill recognized me among the prisoners, invited me outside the corral, to a seat beside him surrounding the public square, where we talked for more than an hour. During the conversation I addressed him once as "Bill"—he very politely requested me to address him as "Captain Quantrill," and took from his pocket and showed me what he claimed was a commission from the Confederate Government, but I did not read it,—being an old acquaintance, and having no grudge against me, he treated me kindly. Not more than a dozen persons were killed on this raid, the object being plunder.

—E.W. Robinson

Softly he speaks,
the taste of peace
between his lips,
the spit from his teeth
calmly meets the ground,
the voice of each man he kills
bleats in this wind
which he has already claimed, shrieks
in the face of this ease
which he has always found,
he leaves the dead slowly,
some do not die but tease him
until he shoots again.
He shoots again. Somewhere,
he knows, there is now, at last,

a cause. This wind is his,
the smell is something else again,
but the wind is finally his,
and the earth, what is that?
Ohio, Kansas, Missouri,
are what? They are names, he says,
they are mine, he thinks,
all names become mine.
I am the ultimate outlaw
of this evil earth.
I am the first and the last
of its new men.
No man will outlive me.

A False Confession

Once there was a man who admitted
that when he was a boy
he admired all prisoners everywhere,
that he would seek out the rooms
they had lived in,
that he might live in them,
that he would think of the earth
as their earth,
that he would imagine cities
as they imagined them.
Once, in winter, the man said,
he walked the roads all night
poorly dressed, groaning against the cold
with the self-assurance that it was strength,
not weakness, to do so.
I do not know where I am going,
the man said, nor why I am going there,
but I go anywhere, I reply to everything,
and they will no more kill me,
these crazy people,
than if I were a corpse already.
In the morning the man looked so lost,
so dead in fact,
that people he met along the way
did not even seem to see him.
Where did he go? they asked.
What was he doing? they wondered.

Once he had a dream of himself
standing before a mob,
it was a firing-squad in fact,
and he cried because
they did not understand him.
You are wrong to turn me in to the law,

the man said, I have never belonged
to you people, I have never understood
your law. I have none of your moral sense,
I know
I am an animal,
and you are making a mistake.
Once he said, I am your Nigger,
I am your beast. You are all
false Niggers, you are the maniacs,
the wild men, you, merchant,
are the Nigger, you, judge,
are the Nigger, you, general,
are the Nigger.
A sickness inspires all these people,
he said, and it would be wise to leave
this new country
where madness
is so prevalent.

Do I not know nature? he asked himself.
Do I not know, even, myself?

No more words, he would then say,
and no more of this civil war.
I will bury the dead in my belly!
Let there be nothing now but
shouting
and dancing and drums
and hunger and thirst and destruction.

I do not see a time yet, he said,
when white men will land here,
and my kind
will fade
into whiteness.

The Raid on Lawrence

Pelathe,
an Indian of the Shawnee,
had heard the news from Bartles,
a Red Leg Scout,
had offered to warn Lawrence,
the city of refuge,
said he would go along the Kansas River,
on the north side,
to avoid the guerillas.
Bartles,
the Red Leg Scout,
said he would never make it in time,
took from the corral his best horse,
a Kentucky sorrel mare,
and Pelathe,
this Indian of the Shawnee,
was off.
It was one o'clock in the morning
and at first he rode slowly,
this Pelathe,
but in an hour, at great speed,
his horse, this Kentucky sorrel mare,
was breathing hard,
so he drew it in for a rest,
took a large red handkerchief
that he wore around his neck,
rubbed its limbs and its flanks
and dried off the sweat.
In the stream he rinsed its mouth
of foam, and gave it water,
until, with its second wind,
they proceeded, this Indian and this horse,
again at great speed, and for several hours,

until, only an hour from Lawrence,
they came to a broad woodland,
where the horse, this sorrel mare,
fell to a slower gait,
then faltered, breathing hard
again, and Pelathe,
who was smart for an Indian,
took out his long knife
and gashed its shoulders,
took gunpowder from his pistol
and rubbed its wounds
until it charged up suddenly,
galloped a few more miles,
then plunged to the ground,
dead.

Pelathe started running down the trail,
came to the cabins of the Delawares,
alarmed them with a war-cry,
stole one of their ponies,
and rode on out for Lawrence.
But it was dawn now,
and Pelathe was, as Bartles said,
too late.
Q. had already entered Lawrence,
                    the city of Lawrence, that is,
                    shining,
                    upon its hill.

        CLANG! BONG!
At the Eldridge House Hotel
a huge gong is struck
to warn the guests who are asleep.
CLANG! BONG! WAKE UP!
Captain Alexander Banks,
the provost marshal of Kansas,
who is a resident of the hotel,
wakes up and waves a sheet from his window

in surrender. Then he calls for Quantrell,
who, lean and handsome and on horseback
rides forward
in a low-crowned, soft, black hat,
a gold cord around it for a band,
cavalry boots and grey trousers,
a brown woolen guerilla's shirt,
and four colt navy pistols in his belt.

And what does he shout?
Kill, he shouts,
kill and you will make no mistake.
Lawrence must be thoroughly cleansed
and the only way to cleanse it
is to kill, he shouts.
As if Lawrence were somehow
the dirtiest of cities
that it must be cleansed so?
—No, that it is only the first
of such cities to be cleansed.

A resident of the town,
who is named Spicer,
leans over the rail of the hotel,
says he remembers Varmint Q.
when he was only Charley Hart.
It doesn't matter, Q. says,
what you call me,
I am going to kill you,
going to burn this hotel,
going to burn this Lawrence,
going to burn this Boston town,
                this city
                shining, so smugly!
                upon its hill!

Senator James H. Lane's residence
is at the northwest corner
of Mississippi and Henry streets.
Q. says later of this man,
"You want to know why I sacked and burned Lawrence,
why I killed all the male population?
It was because I wanted to kill Jim Lane,
the worst man that was ever born into this world.
You want to know what would have been done
with Jim Lane had he been captured?
I would have burned him at the stake!"

127

But Senator James H. Lane hears Quantrell
coming for him, jumps out of bed,
takes the name plate off his door,
runs into a field of corn,
and is safe.
Mrs. James H. Lane asks Quantrell
not to burn her piano with the rest of the house,
and he agrees, but everybody is
too drunk to lift it anyway
once the house is on fire
and it burns too.

>Like a piano
>burning
>upon a hill!
>Hey Paderewski!
>Look there!
>burning
>like a piano
>upon a hill.

The office of the *Tribune*
opposite the Eldridge House:
John Speer, son of the owner,
is asleep in the office,
hears the shots,
sees the raiders in the streets,
runs out the back door,
gets as far as the corner of
Henry and New Hampshire Streets.
There a guerilla demands his money.
This is the Reverend Larkin M. Skaggs
of Cass County, Missouri,
a Baptist minister
who had sacked Lawrence once before,
on May 21, 1856.
When the boy, John Speer,
gives him his money,
the Reverend Skaggs shoots him

and leaves him there for dead.
He lies there ten feet from a building
that is set on fire by three others,
and when the heat becomes unbearable
he begs them to move him
and not let him burn alive.
They shoot him to death and move on.
His brother, Robert Speer, seventeen,
is burned to death in the printshop,
though his mother, Mrs. Speer,
places a dish and a chair at the table
every night for every meal
she ever has in her house after this
until her own death

in the hope that he is still alive
and will come back before the meal is finished
and have dinner.
When William Speer, fifteen,
goes out the door that day
a guerilla asks him his name.
Billy Smith, he says, is my name,
knowing they are checking a list
for anyone with the name of Speer.
And they let him go,
after checking the list
for the name of Smith.
        A city
        shining upon its hill,
        consuming its people
        in flames,
        a Boston city
        shining upon its hill
        in a West that will go,
        now, nowhere.

The raid occurred on the morning of Aug. 21st, 1863. It was a clear, warm, still morning, in the midst of one of the hot, dry, dusty spells of weather common in Kansas in the month of August. The guerillas reached Lawrence just before sunrise after an all night's ride from the border of Missouri. Myself and family were yet in bed and asleep. They passed directly by our house, and we were awakened by their yelling and shouting. I thought at first that the noise came from a company of colored recruits who were camped just west of our house; that they had got to quarreling among themselves. I got up and went to the window to see what was the matter, and as I drew aside the curtain the sight that met my eyes was one of terror—one that I shall never forget. The bush-whackers were just passing by my house. There were 350 of them, all mounted and heavily armed; they were grim and dirty from their night's ride over the dusty roads and were a reckless and bloodthirsty set of men. It was a sight we had somewhat anticipated, felt that it might come, and one that we had dreaded ever since the commencement of the war. I turned to my wife and said: "The bushwhackers are here." They first made for the main street, passing up as far as the Eldridge House to see if they were going to meet with any opposition, and when they found none they scattered out all over the town, killing, stealing and burning. We hastily dressed ourselves and closed up the house tightly as possible and began to talk over what was best to do. My first thought was to get away to some hiding-place, but on looking out there seemed no possibility of that as the enemy were everywhere, and I had a feeling that I ought not to leave my family, a young wife and two children, one a babe of three months old, and so we sat down and awaited developments. We saw men shot down and fires shooting up in all directions.

Just on the north of our house, a half block away and in full view was a camp of recruits twenty-two in all, not yet mustered into service and unarmed. They were awakened by the noise, got up and started to run but were all shot down but five. I saw this wholesale shooting from my window, and it was a sight to strike terror to a stouter heart than mine. But we had not long to wait before our time came. Three of the guerrillas came to the house, stepped up on the front porch, and with the butt of a musket smashed in one of the front windows; my wife opened the door and let them in. They ransacked the house, talked and swore and threatened a good deal, but offered no violence. They set the house on fire above and below, took such things as they fancied, and left. After they had gone I put the fire out below, but above it had got too strong a hold, and I could not put it out.

Not long after a single man rode up to the front gate; he was a villainous looking fellow, and was doubly villainous from too much whiskey. He saw me standing back in the hall of the house, and with a terrible oath he ordered me to come out. I stepped out on the piazza, and he leveled his pistol at me and said; "Are you union or secesh?" It was my time of trial; my wife and her little one in her arms, and our little boy clinging to her side, was standing just a little ways from me. My life seemingly hung on my answer, my position may be imagined but it cannot be described.

131

The thought ran through me like an electric shock, that I could not say that I was a secessionist, and deny my loyalty to my country; that I would rather die than to live and face that disgrace; and so I answered that I was a union man. He snapped his pistol but it failed to fire. I stepped back into the house and he rode around to the north door and met me there, and snapped his pistol at me again, but it failed to fire. Was there a providence in this? Just then a party of a half dozen of the raiders came riding towards the house from the north, and seeing my enemy, hallooed to him "Don't shoot that man." They rode up to the gate and told me to come there; I did so and my would be murderer came up to me and placed the muzzle of his revolver in my ear. It was not a pleasant place to be in, but the leader of the new crowd told him not to shoot; but to let me alone until he could inquire about me, so he asked me if I had ever been down in Missouri stealing niggers or horses; I told him "No, that I never had been in Missouri, except to cross the state going and coming from the east." This seemed to be satisfactory so he told my old enemy to let me alone and not to kill me. This seemed to make him very angry, and he cursed me terribly, but I ventured to put my hand up and push away his revolver. The leader of the party then told me if I did not expect to get killed, I must get out of sight, that they were all getting drunk, and would kill everybody they saw; I told him that that was what I wanted to do all the morning, but I could not; "Well," he says, "you must hide or get killed." And they all rode away. After they had gone I told my wife that I would go into the cellar, and stay until the fire reached me, and if any more of the raiders inquired for me to tell them that I had been taken a prisoner and carried off. Some years ago I read an article in the Sunday School Times, saying that a lie under any circumstances was a sin. I thought then that I should like to see that writer try my experiences at the time of the raid and see what he would think then; I did not feel my lie a sin then and never have since.

But right on
to the Whitney House Hotel

he moves, this Varmint, Q.,
William Clarke Quantrell
must have his breakfast!
He has it with the owner
of the Whitney House Hotel
whose name is Stone.
They are old friends.
They discuss old times.
Q. is a man only
27 years old
but such a man has had
old times too,
or thinks he has
had such times
            —a few cities
            —a few friends
            —a few beers

It is a rare case of a future old time,
the burning of Lawrence,
still in the making,
still a new time,
but there is always time to talk,
and in that way, over coffee in the present,
the present becomes the past,
becomes the old time,
and the old time then never recedes
from the new and . . .

Such a man is ageless, he thinks,
and the ageless are, of course,
dangerous.

After breakfast at the Whitney House Hotel,
Q. takes a buggy and rides through the streets,
canters over the dead,
the buildings burning around him.
He rides to the top of Mount Oread

where he gets out of the buggy
and looks down on the city below
                   a man
                   shining now
                   upon a hill,
                   a city
                   beneath the man
                   in flames
(As violets,
            they say,
are the food of spiders

while a fly is dissolved
by a sunbeam
                   what light
penetrates
this city
                   morning
                         breakfast
                               hour?

            This place
that eats raw
the day
            the hour
                   the century?
Everything
is out of an ordinary
that never really was

            And a crunch
you cannot even hear
                   swallows
the image in the mirror . . .
Oh come on!
This is not the time
for lyric and rhyme.
A song and dance maybe—

liar, liar
　　your pants are on fire—
to liven up the deadliness
of every man's disorder.
Just tell the story.
Only the story is
the whole poem!
Just tell the poem.)

                    This time
the Reverend Larkin M. Skaggs
stops at the house of Fred W. Read,
and when Mrs. Read answers the door,
he says, "I have come to make a call."
When Mrs. Read answers the door, she says,
"I am not receiving any calls."
So the Reverend Larkin M. Skaggs says
he will burn down the house
and he asks Mrs. Read for a box of matches.
She refuses to give him any matches
but he finds them, and he lights one,
but Mrs. Read immediately blows it out,
so he lights another, which she also blows out,
and another, and for ten minutes
Mrs. Read continues to blow his matches out.
"You are the queerest woman I ever saw,"
says the Reverend Larkin M. Skaggs,
and he takes out his gun to shoot her,
but suddenly he realizes
that all the other guerillas
have already left Lawrence,
so he mounts his horse and leaves
her house.
                    In hesitation,
                    upon the hill,
                    that the city
                                is
                    no longer there
                    A man in isolation,
                    dull and
                    deceived by
                    what? by the many?
                    by the city itself!

When William Speer, fifteen,
finally gets home, his mother gives him a gun
and says to go out and shoot some guerillas.

He goes out and shoots
the Reverend Larkin M. Skaggs
and knocks him from his horse.
When the Reverend Larkin M. Skaggs
falls from his horse,
a Delaware Indian, whose name is
White Turkey, runs up,
says, "Him kill everybody,
me kill him," and he scalps
the Reverend Larkin M. Skaggs
who becomes the only guerilla killed
in the whole Lawrence raid.
When C. M. Chase rides into town
later that day, the first thing he sees is
a black man rushing through the streets
on horseback, dragging the body of
the Reverend Larkin M. Skaggs
behind him with a rope around his neck,
while a crowd pelts the body with stones.
An attempt, later, to burn the body,
fails, and the bones lay all winter
in a ravine in the town,
where boys saw off the finger rings
and where no part of the man
is interred.

> Pollution!
> That is what it is!
> The stink
> of this city
> rotting
> upon its hill.
> The filth
> of this city
> stinking
> upon a hill!

As all cities
everywhere
thereafter
in this land,
some will say,
but this was a first
of a sort,

was it not?
And Lawrence,
like the West itself,
was an end,
not some imaginary
beginning.

Unburied bodies
in its sewers,
Lawrence creates
the primal American nightmare Main Street mind,
and Q. only executes
its favors,
only performs his
"heroism"
at the town's expense,
as some will say
of those who do it
thereafter,
as if
a hero is only a man
who breaks a law
that nobody knew
was there.

But Q.,
you are a lunatic, too,
and they will kill you now,
a city is despoiled,
a hundred and fifty citizens

are dead,
And there is no appeal
from that.
And the city of Lawrence is, now,
like the Earth itself!
made in a morning—
this morning—
       to shine so
              completely
       upon its hill.

The Death of Varmint Q.

This is the poem
of a man named Quantrell:
it begins,
"My horse
is at the door,
the enemy
I soon may see."
You see,
there was a horse,
whose name was Charley,
the horse of
William Clarke Quantrell,
whose friends said
of this horse
that it so absorbed
the nature
of its master (Quantrell),
that the horse had become
a guerrilla,
that is, the best guard
in camp, they said,
who sounded the alarm
many times, but
this horse
(whose name was Charley)
became vicious,
and no one but
William Clarke Quantrell
could control him.
He would bite and kick
and quarrel with
everyone else.

William Clarke Quantrell
alone
rode this horse.
To shoe him,
you had to
tie him up,
and one day, Jack Graham, who,
along with the horse

had also become a guerrilla,
was shoeing him, using
a buttress,
when the horse
struggled so
it became hamstrung
and so, ruined,
and when they finally told
William Clarke Quantrell
of this accident,
he recoiled
as though he were
shot, killed,
then he said, halting,
my work is done,
my career is run,
death is coming
and my end is near.
(This was not part
of the poem of the man).
But he did write a poem,
this man,
and the poem did say,
"Here's a sigh
to those who love me,
and a smile
to those who hate."
But as one of those
who hated this man
was a man named Lincoln,
William Clarke Quantrell decided
he was to be next
on his list, and last,
this man, this Lincoln,
who lived in Washington:
they would ride into Washington,
all these guerrilla men,
and they would shoot this

Lincoln.
Everybody said,
it couldn't be done,
because, you see,
it never had been,
and so it wasn't,
by this man,
by William Clarke Quantrell,
who rode into
Kentucky instead.
But then this other man,
this Lincoln, *was* shot,
and William Clarke Quantrell
decided to hold
a toast! and said,
"The grand-daddy of all
the greenbacks
is dead, Abraham Lincoln,
in a theater, was shot,
so here's
to the death
of Abraham Lincoln."
And his poem went on,
"In this verse,
as with the wine,
the libation I would pour,"
and you see there was
a libation that would be poured,
on a farm, in Kentucky,
at the house of a man
whose name was
Wakefield.
(It was at the house
of a lady,
whose name was
Dawson,
that he wrote
this poem.)

It was only a few days later
when a man
whose name was
Terrill,
rode into Wakefield
with his men
and shot this man,
this William Clarke Quantrell.
This man Terrill
had been a *Confederate* officer,
and only nineteen years old
when a major general
of the Union,
whose name was
John Palmer,
commissioned him
to be a guerrilla
for the *Union* side
and to shoot this man,
this Quantrell.
It was raining that day
and Quantrell was asleep
in a barn in a loft of hay
when this man, this Terrill,
rode in with his men
and started shooting
and so the man ran out
of the barn
and was shot
down
in the back by a bullett
that entered
at the end
of the left
shoulder blade
struck the spine
and paralyzed him,
when another shot then

after he fell
cut off the trigger
finger
of his right hand.
The man whose name was
Terrill, and his men,
took off the boots
of the man whose name was
Quantrell,
and some even took other
trophies,
and though the man offered them
his gold watch
and five hundred dollars
if they would let him go,
they would not
let him go,
they did not, until the man
whose name was
Wakefield
gave the man, Terrill,
twenty dollars
and a jug of whiskey
if they would desist
and take him to the house,
which they did,
where a doctor was called,
who said it was
hopeless.
Then it was May 12th, 1865,
and the man was moved to
Louisville,
to a military prison,
where when it was June 16th, 1865
he died.
But two young ladies,
whose names were

Maggie Frederick
and Sallie Lovell,
had sent the man a bouquet,
marked,
"With the compliments
of Miss Maggie Frederick
and Sallie Lovell
to Mr. Quantrill."

(And this too was not
a part of the poem,
because it rhymed.)
But the poem of this man
went on, and said,
"Though the cannons
roar
around me,
yet it still
shall bear me on."

Louisville Daily Democrat, JUNE 7, 1865
Captain Terrill and his company arrived here yesterday from
Taylorsville. They brought with them the guerrilla who bears the
name of "Quantrill." It is not the Quantrill of Kansas notoriety,
for we have been assured that he was at last accounts a colonel
in rebel army under Price. This prisoner was shot through the
body in a fight in a barn near Taylorsville on Wednesday last.
Five others were killed on the spot by Terrill's men, but what
their names were we could not ascertain. The prisoner brought
down is confined in the military prison hospital and is said to
be in a dying condition.

And you see, the man
did die,
though the people
could not be sure
(the people
would never be sure),
because the poem of the man
went on
and on.
It was the poem of a man
named Quantrell.

147